Harvard
Business
Review

on

FIXING
HEALTH CARE
FROM
INSIDE & OUT

The Harvard Business Review
Paperback series

If you need the best practices and ideas for the business challenges you face—but don't have time to find them—*Harvard Business Review* paperbacks are for you. Each book is a collection of HBR's inspiring and useful perspectives on a given management topic, all in one place.

The titles include:

Harvard Business Review on Advancing Your Career
Harvard Business Review on Aligning Technology with Strategy
Harvard Business Review on Building Better Teams
Harvard Business Review on Collaborating Effectively
Harvard Business Review on Communicating Effectively
Harvard Business Review on Finding & Keeping the Best People
Harvard Business Review on Fixing Health Care from Inside & Out
Harvard Business Review on Greening Your Business Profitably
Harvard Business Review on Increasing Customer Loyalty
Harvard Business Review on Inspiring & Executing Innovation
Harvard Business Review on Making Smart Decisions
Harvard Business Review on Managing Supply Chains
Harvard Business Review on Rebuilding Your Business Model
Harvard Business Review on Reinventing Your Marketing
Harvard Business Review on Succeeding as an Entrepreneur
Harvard Business Review on Thriving in Emerging Markets
Harvard Business Review on Winning Negotiations

Harvard Business Review

on

FIXING HEALTH CARE FROM INSIDE & OUT

Harvard Business Review Press

Boston, Massachusetts

Library of Congress Cataloging-in-Publication Data

Harvard business review on fixing health care from inside & out.
    p. ; cm.—(Harvard business review paperback series)
    ISBN 978-1-4221-6258-3 (alk. paper)
    1. Medical care—United States.   2. Health care reform—United States.
I. Harvard Business School.   II. Harvard business review.   III. Series:
Harvard business review paperback series.
    [DNLM: 1. Delivery of Health Care—trends—United States.
2. Health Care Reform—United States. W 84 AA1]
    RA395.A3H3814   2011
    362.1'0425—dc22

                                                        2011000834

Contents

**Harvard
Business
Review**

on

FIXING
HEALTH CARE
FROM
INSIDE & OUT

Turning Doctors into Leaders

by Thomas H. Lee

THE PROBLEM WITH HEALTH CARE is people like me—doctors (mostly men) in our fifties and beyond, who learned medicine when it was more art and less finance. We were taught to go to the hospital before dawn, stay until our patients were stable, focus on the needs of each patient before us, and not worry about costs. We were taught to review every test result with our own eyes—to depend on no one. The only way to ensure quality was to adopt high personal standards for ourselves and then meet them. Now, at many health care institutions and practices, we are in charge. And that's a problem, because health care today needs a fundamentally different approach—and a new breed of leaders.

Most recent discussions of health care have focused on its rising costs, but these financial challenges are really just a symptom. What is the real "disease"? The usual suspects have surprisingly small roles. Greed and incompetence surely exist, but economists agree that they don't account for double-digit annual cost increases on their own.

The good and the bad news is that the biggest driver of rising costs is medical progress: new drugs, new tests, new devices, and new ways of using them. These tools are frequently marvelous and complex, and their use requires increasing numbers of personnel trained in narrow fields. Patients with complicated conditions end up seeing a variety of physicians who are often spread across several institutions.

Of course this progress is welcome, and at times it seems miraculous. The Red Sox pitcher Jon Lester was diagnosed with lymphoma in September 2006, but he reported to spring training in 2007 and pitched a no-hitter in 2008. Steve Jobs is still on the job. Many patients diagnosed with heart failure can now go back to work after receiving a new type of high-tech pacemaker.

But this explosion of knowledge is going off within a system too fragmented and disorganized to absorb it. The result is chaos. In my own organization, Partners HealthCare, a poignant example involves the widow of a young man who died of cancer. In the last days of his final six-week stay in the intensive care unit, she demanded that all his doctors have a meeting with the family. The family didn't really need the meeting, she said—the doctors did. She wanted to be sure that the various physicians were actually talking to one another, because she so often received inconsistent or even contradictory messages from them. The confusion she described does more than distress families, of course. It leads to redundant care and errors that raise costs and threaten quality.

Idea in Brief

The problem with medicine, the author writes, is people like him: Fifty-something doctors trained in an era of autonomous hero-practitioners. These lone cowboy physicians may work hard, but they don't provide the best possible care, because they're embedded in a fragmented, chaotic, performance-blind system. Fixing this will require a new kind of leader who can organize doctors into teams, measure their performance not by how much they do but by how their patients fare, deftly apply financial and behavioral incentives, improve processes, and dismantle dysfunctional cultures. Drawing on examples from best-practice institutions such as the Cleveland Clinic, Seattle's Virginia Mason Medical Center, Intermountain Healthcare in Utah, and his own organization, Partners HealthCare System of Boston, Lee shows how a "new breed of leader" is orienting strategy around patients' needs (a more radical idea than it might sound) and raising the quality, efficiency, and value of care. A sidebar written by Partners strategy director Kelly W. Hall looks at how peer pressure can drive improved performance.

Tough Medicine

To effectively attack this chaos we need a new kind of leadership at every level of the health care system, from large integrated delivery systems like Partners to hospitals to physician practices. The specific kinds of work and performance measures may differ from one setting to another, but the key responsibilities of leadership are the same. To understand what they are, leaders must first absorb three painful messages.

Performance Matters

Most clinicians are hard workers, but the quality of their work should not be measured by how many patients they manage to see or tests and procedures they call for.

What matters is their results. This is controversial, because comparing outcomes is notoriously complicated. After all, how well patients eventually do depends heavily on how sick they were to start with. Nonetheless, the bottom line is how patients fare. How often do they survive their illnesses and recover from their disabilities? How frequently do they get infections and other complications? Are their informational and emotional needs met?

"Value" Is Not a Bad Word

When employers and insurance companies use the term, many providers suspect that it's code for cost reduction. But Michael Porter, of Harvard Business School, and others have been pointing out for years that in health care, "value" means something else: achieving good outcomes as efficiently as possible. It may never be expressible as a numerical ratio (quality divided by costs) that allows meaningful comparisons among providers. But measuring outcomes and costs does allow providers to push for improvement—and to learn from their competitors.

Improvements in Performance Require Teamwork

Individual clinicians and hospitals have only limited control over the fate of their patients. At any organization that provides health care, superior coordination, information sharing, and teamwork across disciplines are required if value and outcomes are to improve.

Many leaders of providers can pinpoint the moment when they realized that their world was changing; often it came when someone outside the organization started measuring its performance. Although few providers welcome this development, it provides context for a new breed of leaders. Traditional health care leaders try to buy time, fend off change, and maximize revenue under the existing payment system while they can. The new leaders focus on outcomes and use performance measurement as a motivating tool to organize their colleagues and drive improvements.

The challenges are similar whether these leaders are working in a large integrated delivery system, a hospital, a large multispecialty physician group, or a small physician practice. Although their tactics will vary from one setting to the next, the broad roles that leaders need to assume will not.

Articulating Vision and Values

The reorganization process starts with articulating the rationale and goals for change. Change is hard in any field, and medicine's altruistic core values actually reinforce practitioners' resistance to disturbing the status quo. My generation's traditionalists know that they are good people who work hard, and they have the courage of their convictions as they point out the risks of change. So the vision expressed by leaders in health care must convey both understanding and resolve. It should acknowledge the importance of what clinicians currently do, but make explicit that they have to work differently in the future. It should be direct about the measures by which they must succeed. And it should be both optimistic and realistic, expressing the beliefs that care can get better and that delivering superior care is the best business strategy.

An effective vision helps people accept inevitable changes and put information and events into context. For example, many physicians and hospital leaders have a viscerally negative reaction to public reporting on the quality of care they provide. They know the limitations of the data and are appalled that providers might be ranked numerically on the basis of inadequate, easily misinterpreted information. Their typical reaction to a decision to release data on provider quality: Civilization is coming to an end.

In contrast, consider how the cardiac surgeon Delos M. Cosgrove, who became CEO of the Cleveland Clinic in 2004, folded the imperative for performance measurement into a broad vision. If the clinic was committed to the idea of "patients first," he argued, it had to not only make a serious commitment to measuring patient outcomes but also demonstrate that commitment to the world. Cosgrove immediately took the measurement systems that had evolved in one part of the organization and disseminated them throughout the clinic. At first the new data were available only to insiders; now they are published, warts and all, on the clinic's website. Physicians were indeed uncomfortable with these changes, but seeing performance measurement as a tool to help (and attract) patients, rather than as just a carrot or a stick, brought them along.

Leaders at Seattle's Virginia Mason Medical Center made a similar commitment to the notion of patients first, but they took it a step further by making explicit its clear corollary: Physicians and everyone else come second. Whereas patients in most cancer centers do the walking—to the laboratory, to doctors' offices, to chemotherapy infusion rooms—patients visiting Virginia Mason's new cancer center are ushered into well-appointed rooms where doctors, nurses, and lab technicians come to them. These rooms are filled with natural light from large windows; the physicians work in windowless cubicles in the floor's interior.

Virginia Mason's cancer center embraced its patients-first vision so zealously that some of the doctors on the staff left. But those who remained, despite some grumbling, have helped engineer the center's financial turnaround and rise to national prominence.

Organizing for Performance

Focusing on performance in health care is more radical than it sounds. In the era now waning, the conventional wisdom has been that true quality can't be measured. Thus performance has generally been gauged by the volume and profitability of services delivered.

In the traditional world, medicine is organized around what doctors do rather than what patients need. For example, hospitals often have separate units for cardiology, cardiac surgery, cardiac anesthesiology, and radiology, each of which includes doctors and other clinicians who contribute to the care of patients with heart disease. Every unit has a physician leader and an administrative staff. At many hospitals the various units independently submit their bills ("claims") to insurance companies and patients. That's why patients are so often confused by multiple bills.

These clinicians may actually work well together in caring for individual patients, but increased costs and dysfunction are inherent in separated administrative structures. The units are staffed by people with good intentions, but they all have turf to defend—and in the mainstream of American medicine, threatening someone's turf is a quick path to destructive conflict. In the absence of compelling reasons to change this arrangement, inefficient structures remain stubbornly in place. And for clinicians to embrace a radical redesign of care delivery—well, that would be an unnatural act when they are organized according to their specialties and contented to remain so.

This fragmentation often goes deeper than the organizational division of physicians. At many hospitals relationships between doctors and administrators are downright antagonistic, and financial interests are poorly aligned or even in direct conflict. For instance, hospitals want to shorten lengths of stay because they receive a lump sum for a patient's entire admission, but doctors are paid for each visit on each hospital day, so the sooner patients go home, the less they make. Under most insurance plans, neither is rewarded for doing the extra work that might prevent a readmission to the hospital.

Organizing to deliver high performance (rather than units of service) can help break down all these barriers. As performance starts to matter, for example, some providers are moving toward structures for the delivery of care that are defined by patients' needs. In many cases, the first step is colocation—putting the various types of physicians who provide most of the care for a patient population in one place. Sometimes an opportunity for colocation is created by the construction of a new facility dedicated to patients with specific conditions, such as cardiac disease or cancer. More often, institutional leaders must move groups around in an elaborate multiyear effort to bring physicians from different disciplines but the same patient population closer to one another.

But colocation alone can't guarantee a well-coordinated effort to improve patient outcomes. That's why Delos Cosgrove abolished the Cleveland Clinic's traditional departments and replaced them with "institutes" defined by patients' conditions. He realized that as a cardiac surgeon, he needed to collaborate more with cardiologists than with surgeons who operated on other parts of the body. So he brought together the clinic's cardiologists, cardiac surgeons, and vascular surgeons in the new Heart and Vascular Institute, and started capturing and publishing information on how its patients have fared.

In similar facilities, such as the Head and Neck Center at Houston's M.D. Anderson Cancer Center, physicians remain members of their various departments, but they're in close proximity on two adjacent floors. Over time they have come to identify more with their cancer-center roles than with their departmental affiliations.

Rule of thumb

Generally speaking, the number of people an organization needs to train in process improvement is the square root of the total number of personnel.

Thus, if you have 100 people, you need to train 10; if you have 10,000, you need to train 100. Most organizations have a long way to go to reach this goal.

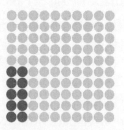

The work of organizing care around the needs of patients instead of physicians' turf and politics plays out on smaller scales as well. Within many leading hospitals today, physicians from the departments of surgery, medicine, and radiology work together to perform hybrid procedures (such as simultaneous open-heart surgery and abdominal aneurysm repair) that previously would have been performed separately.

Large-scale organizational changes like these require strong leaders and a cultural context in which they can lead. For obvious reasons, such leaders gain additional leverage if they are physicians and their organization employs its doctors. At the Cleveland Clinic all physicians are on one-year renewable contracts, which sends a powerful message about the importance of team spirit.

Not every institution will have the leadership wherewithal to undertake such transformative change. But even when integrating departments of clinicians seems unrealistic, strategically chosen performance measures can spur progress.

Developing a Measurement System

The first challenge in creating a performance measurement system is getting everyone across an organization to use the same "language"—that is, to measure the same things in the same way. Otherwise it's easy, and understandable, for resisters to challenge the validity of apparent differences. But once providers believe that apples are being accurately compared with apples, peer pressure and other incentives will help spread best practices. (See the sidebar "Using Peer Pressure to Improve Performance.")

Consider this example of the importance of a common language, which comes from my own organization. Bloodstream infections are a serious and frequent problem in patients who have indwelling catheters in their arteries and veins, and in January 2008 the Massachusetts state government announced plans to begin public reporting of each hospital's rate of such infections. Knowing that reporting was coming, my colleagues began including data on bloodstream infections in the internal quality report cards that are shared with our board and other senior leaders. These reports

Using Peer Pressure to Improve Performance

by Kelly W. Hall

FINANCIAL INCENTIVES IN HEALTH CARE, as in any other industry, are necessary but not sufficient to optimize people's performance. If, for instance, they are linked to too many or very complex targets, or if the performance standard is unrealistically high, their effect is blunted. In the worst case, physicians just throw their hands in the air and ignore them, viewing the pain of achieving the targets as greater than the potential gain.

Peer pressure can provide incentives that financial rewards can't. As one group-practice medical director put it, "Doctors are very competitive and want to be A students, so I use those two characteristics as levers to motivate behavior change." When providers are shown data on measures such as infection rates, hospital readmissions, diabetes control, and test utilization—especially if their own performance falls short and colleagues can see it—they will often try to improve simply as a matter of professional pride. But for peer pressure to work, group members must have a fundamental respect for the integrity of the performance data. Otherwise the data may fuel anger and recrimination rather than improvement. For example, if an organization's physicians react to confidential performance reports with skepticism and denial, their responses to similar data presented publicly are likely to be even more extreme. Or if discussions of other practice-related matters quickly devolve into argument, that's probably a sign that the group isn't ready to handle the emotionally charged issue of comparative performance.

Many physician groups within Partners HealthCare combine peer pressure and financial incentives. At Hawthorn Medical Associates, a large multispecialty group near New Bedford, Massachusetts, physicians know exactly how they compare with their peers, both locally and across the network, on specific pay-for-performance measures. Those with the lowest rankings meet with medical directors to discuss strategies for improvement. Those with high rankings are invited to comment on the data and suggest reasons for their success. All data are presented to the practice in a group setting, with doctors' names clearly visible.

One performance report showed dramatic variation across a group of physicians in their use of radiology tests such as CAT scans and MRIs. When faced with such data, Hawthorn's medical director says, doctors' reactions "can be anything on the Kübler-Ross spectrum from anger to denial to resignation." To mitigate negative effects, he follows up immediately with physicians to tell them exactly how they might improve. "That way," he says, "it isn't just sharing bad news but giving people hope and something to work on . . . and gently reminding them that similar data will be shared during next month's meeting." In this group radiology test use fell by 15% in the first year and has held steady since. These physicians have also made progress in diabetes management and clinical outcomes using a similar approach.

Charles River Medical Associates, a 50-physician multispecialty group outside Boston, takes the combination of peer pressure and financial incentives to an even higher level. Each physician is assessed approximately $10,000 a year to create an internal incentive pool for promoting various elements of "citizenship." For one element—patient satisfaction—the group uses data to rank physicians from top to bottom and shares the results with the whole group. Financially, it's a zero-sum game: Those who score above average receive a bonus, and those who score below average pay a tax. The further a physician is from the mean, the more money is at stake.

The typical response to the ranking list is "a bunch of e-mails and calls from the people at the bottom," according to Charles River's practice administrator. But ultimately, he says, "they want to know why they're bad and what they can do to fix it."

Kelly W. Hall (khall@pchi.partners.org) is the executive director of strategic planning at Partners Community HealthCare in Boston.

revealed apparent differences in the rates at two of our hospitals, but meaningful comparisons were hindered by their differing methods of detecting the infections.

Hospital A monitored for infections by drawing blood samples through the indwelling catheters—an approach that was painless and easy but more likely to lead to contamination or false positives. Hospital B checked for infections by drawing blood through fresh needle sticks. Hospital A usually had higher rates of infection, but its physicians always argued that this was simply a false finding resulting from their particular detection method. After they finally adopted Hospital B's method, however, they found that they still had a higher infection rate. With both hospitals measuring in the same way, claims about the source of the difference ended. Infection-control leaders became very interested in what else Hospital B did differently.

When data are uniform and reliable, leaders can push for the standardization of best practices throughout an organization. For example, clinicians at all the hospitals in our system have agreed to attach colored tape to catheters inserted under less-than-ideal conditions in the emergency department. The tape tells doctors and nurses in the intensive care unit to change those lines as soon as possible once the patient is stable—a practice that we expect will further reduce our infection rates.

In this case, standards were not dictated from the top of the organization. What did come from the top was pressure to collect data in the same way at all hospitals and use it to improve care. Innovation occurs at the front lines of health care; our senior managers would never have thought of using colored tape on catheters. But they could and did create the environment in which such ideas spread.

Finally, an effective measurement system requires clear metrics that detail costs and outcomes for episodes of care or even entire patient populations. These data can be wielded in ways of varying impact. Although workers in any environment, medical or otherwise, will respond to negative motivators ("Reduce the infection rate or you will be humiliated"), positive ones ("Reduce the rate because you want to provide the best possible care") can be more effective. Such value-oriented performance measurement should become the focus of internal improvement efforts—before measurement is forced upon leaders from the outside.

Building Effective Teams

Working in teams does not come easily to physicians, who still often see themselves as heroic lone healers. Nonetheless, developing teams is a key leadership function for health care providers of all types.

Consider how teams at Pennsylvania's Geisinger Health System (where I sit on the board) have helped cut hospital readmissions by half. In the United States about 20% of Medicare patients discharged from the hospital are readmitted within 30 days. These "bouncebacks" should be seen for what they are—failures of the delivery system to meet patients' needs. Even in retrospect many readmissions seem unpreventable, but others result from confusion about what medicines the patient should be taking, what signs might suggest that a complication is brewing, when the patient should go back to which doctor, and so on.

In that confusion lies an opportunity for well-organized providers. The obvious ingredient in Geisinger's recipe for success is placing nurses ("care coordinators") in the offices of patients' primary-care physicians. The care coordinators stay in close touch with patients whose cases are complex, particularly when they are about to be discharged from the hospital or have recently gone home. They figure out which patients need to see which physicians and when.

The more subtle ingredient in this model's success—the secret sauce, as it were—is a culture in which care coordinators can actually coordinate care. It requires that physicians be both team leaders and team players. Not long ago, in the strict hierarchy of medicine, nurses were largely regarded as technicians whose job was to follow orders. No decision was made without a physician's knowledge and consent. The notion of a nurse as a critical contributor and independent decision maker on a clinical team would have seemed absurd.

That's changing, because providers that deliver care in the traditional way simply can't match the performance of Geisinger and other organizations where physicians work in teams with care coordinators. In these organizations the coordinator's role is something like that of a point guard in basketball, with the physician acting as a combined general manager and player-coach. Leading these teams requires physicians to hand off considerable responsibility to nurses. The payoff is improved performance on the metrics that matter most to them and their patients.

Team building is a critical competency for leaders of physician groups, particularly the increasingly common groups of 25 or more that include doctors from a range of specialties. Most of these doctors joined their groups not because they wanted to work collaboratively with others to improve performance but because they wanted to be in a big organization where someone else would worry about administrative hassles, they'd find some safety in numbers from market forces, and it would be possible to make additional revenue from ancillary services such as radiology and laboratory testing.

But the fortunes of these groups and others in all areas of medicine will depend on leaders who can improve performance by inspiring (or requiring) teamwork. In many markets insurers are incorporating costs and quality in insurance product design, so that patients pay more—or aren't covered at all—if they want to see physicians in more-expensive, less-efficient, or lower-quality groups. If patients don't come, the groups will fail. The ability to build high-performance teams confers competitive advantage.

Improving Processes

Health care teams can't view their purpose as time-limited or focused on one project. The day will never come when readmission rates are low enough, heart-attack treatment is fast enough, or all the processes of care delivery are efficient and reliable enough. Thus leaders must work relentlessly to reduce errors and waste and improve outcomes—for example, by preventing bounce-backs or reducing the time between a heart-attack patient's arrival in the emergency room and the opening of his or her blocked artery. To do so they need a culture of process improvement and the disciplined use of its methods, such as lean management, data collection, brainstorming, intervention, and impact analysis—and a long-term commitment to applying them. That culture and experience can be ingrained in a variety of ways.

The now classic health care example comes from Virginia Mason Medical Center, which a decade ago was in danger of losing market share and its best physicians to the numerous outstanding hospitals in the region. In 2001 the center's president, J. Michael Rona, happened to sit next to John Black, then the director of lean management at Boeing, on a plane. Black had sent hundreds of Boeing managers to Japan to study the Toyota Production System. By the end of his flight, Rona was convinced that Virginia Mason needed to do the same thing.

Rona and the center's CEO, a physician named Gary Kaplan, began taking groups of their colleagues to Japan for two-week immersion courses in TPS. Rona and Kaplan let it be known across the organization that leadership roles would most likely be reserved for people (including physicians) who took the training and adopted the lessons. Some of their star physicians left as a result. But Virginia Mason has used its version of

TPS to reduce costs, improve quality and service, and strengthen its financial health.

Of course, not all hospitals or practices can or should fly their staff to Japan. But they can find (and increasingly are finding) alternative ways to bring the process-improvement culture inside. Many organizations have sent their midlevel and senior leaders for training at Intermountain Healthcare in Utah, where Brent James, the chief quality officer, runs a highly respected process-improvement course. And James has generously helped some of these organizations, including mine, start their own courses to spread this expertise.

Dismantling Cultural Barriers

Why is collaboration so hard in a field that attracts idealistic people who want to do good? Why are performance measurement and improvement so problematic for some of the smartest, hardest-working, and most competitive people in society? Why is the concept of value rejected by providers that would benefit if they improved their care?

In a word, autonomy. The cultural barriers to change in health care—doctors' resistance to being measured, their need be "perfect," their reluctance to criticize colleagues, their resistance to teamwork—reflect a deep-seated belief that physician autonomy is crucial to quality in health care. Doctors have historically seen themselves as their patients' sole advocates, with the rest of the world divided into those who are helping and those who are in the way. A temper tantrum in the pursuit of patients' interests was acceptable behavior. Some of my most respected colleagues have confessed a wish that no one would even talk to their patients except through them.

Precious as this passion for patients' interests might be, physician autonomy is not synonymous with quality. For the needed structural and operational changes—performance measurement, process improvement, teamwork—to become mainstream, doctors must accept that to be all-caring is different from being all-knowing or all-controlling. To foster such acceptance, leaders can use three approaches.

Appeal to the Better Angels

People who are drawn to health care want to focus their life's work on something good: helping patients. Altruism is core to the identity of physicians and virtually everyone else in medicine. Health care leaders cannot succeed without making it explicit that they share and will act on the same aspiration.

Twice during the past several years I watched James J. Mongan, the recently retired CEO of Partners Health-Care, sit quietly while colleagues discussed whether to make a given practice standard across our network of physicians. The first time was January 6, 2005, when we considered whether to mandate the use of electronic medical records. The second was March 6, 2007, when we weighed automatically enrolling patients with heart failure in a disease management program, as opposed to waiting for physicians to refer them.

We believed that both steps would improve patient care, but we hesitated because we knew we'd anger some physicians by curtailing their autonomy. They might leave our network and take their referrals with them. In both instances, though, Mongan brought the discussion to an end by saying, "I really think this is the right thing to do." No one could argue with him, and no one did. In medicine, more than in most other fields, a senior leader's appeal to doing "the right thing" can serve as a trump card.

Show Them the Data
Physicians are quick to challenge performance data and to identify methodological problems with them. But the fact is that they are mesmerized by data and cannot look away. Brent James may be the ultimate health care data swami; for decades he has put the collection and sharing of data on quality and efficiency at the core of Intermountain Healthcare's culture. Rather than make a frontal attack on physicians' autonomy, he wears down their resistance to change by showing them how their practice varies from the norm.

Define Strategy Around Patients' Needs
What doctors know and do is constantly changing, but the needs of patients remain the same. They get diseases, they worry, and they hope to be cured or relieved of suffering. Meeting their needs is what health care is about. As we've seen, the leaders of organizations like the Cleveland Clinic, Intermountain Healthcare, and Virginia Mason Medical Center have taken the concept

of patients first from an abstraction to a robust organizational strategy.

A shift to value-oriented, performance-driven health care requires doctors to adapt or even reject some ways of working that are embedded in medicine's past. Difficult as this change will be, I am optimistic that the new generation of leaders will achieve it. In truth, they have no choice. Defending the status quo is no longer a viable strategy, even in the near term.

THOMAS H. LEE is the network president of Partners HealthCare System, in Boston, and a professor of medicine at Harvard Medical School.

Originally published in April 2010. Reprint R1004B

Health Care Needs a New Kind of Hero

An Interview with Atul Gawande
by Gardiner Morse

IN HIS LATEST BOOK, *The Checklist Manifesto,* surgeon and writer Atul Gawande describes how asking some simple questions before surgery starts—such as "Did we give the patient her antibiotic?" and even "Did we introduce ourselves to one another?"—can reduce infections and deaths by more than a third. Easy as this exercise is, it's often met with hostility, because it challenges doctors' cherished notions about status, autonomy, and expertise. In this edited interview, HBR senior editor Gardiner Morse asks Gawande what checklists reveal about the culture of medicine and how its dysfunctions might be fixed.

HBR: *Despite doctors' resistance to new ideas, surgical checklists are gaining a foothold. What does that tell us about how to speed up other changes in health care?*

Atul Gawande: If you try to impose a new practice by simply telling the front line "Do this," it will fail. That's particularly true for something like a checklist, which many surgeons at first felt was beneath them. To get people to embrace a practice, it has to be easy and quick to use, adaptable to a variety of settings, and of obvious benefit. In hospital after hospital, checklists reduced mistakes and saved lives, and clinicians who used them saw greater efficiency and teamwork, which made them willing to continue using them. My operating room finishes up earlier in the day than others, which is one reason people like our checklists. The other crucial thing is having senior people who practice what they preach. When we piloted checklists in hospitals around the world, we asked the chiefs of surgery, anesthesiology, and nursing to be the first people to use them.

Health care is moving toward teams, but that collides with the image of the all-knowing, heroic lone healer.

That's right. We've celebrated cowboys, but what we need is more pit crews. There's still a lot of silo mentality in health care—the mentality of "That's not my problem; someone else will take care of it"—and that's very dangerous.

How do we move toward a culture where effective teams are the norm?

Part of the answer is a change in medical training. Most medicine is delivered by teams of people, with the physician, in theory, the team captain. Yet we don't train physicians how to lead teams or be team

Idea in Brief

The surgeon and best-selling author readily concedes his own limitations as he explains how doctors—and health care generally—could do better. In his latest book, *The Checklist Manifesto*, Atul Gawande describes how asking a set of simple questions before the surgery starts—things like "Did we give the patient her antibiotic?" and even "Did we introduce ourselves to one another?"—can reduce infections and deaths by nearly half. As simple as this exercise is, it's often met with hostility, because it challenges beloved notions about doctors' status, autonomy, and expertise. In this edited interview Gawande discusses what checklists reveal about the culture of medicine and how its dysfunctions might be fixed.

members. This should begin in medical school. One of the most fascinating experiments along these lines is at the University of Nevada at Reno, where the schools of medicine and nursing have combined facilities and courses. Doctors and nurses in training are learning how to work together. It's a brand-new thing.

But simply training people in team techniques isn't enough, is it? To get effective collaboration, don't you have to change doctors' self-image?

The stories we doctors tell ourselves about what it means to be great are very important to who we are, but they create a cognitive dissonance. We like to imagine we can be infallible and be that heroic healer. But the fact is, it's teams and, often, great organizations that make for great care, not just individuals. So we need to change these stories we tell ourselves and reshape the discussion.

How can you do that?

Well, for instance, when you use a checklist in the OR, there's a moment when you ask all the people in the room to introduce themselves by name. That's been the source of the greatest resistance, actually. It seems hokey. But when you do it, people say, "I'm Bob, the anesthesiologist; I'm Susan, the anesthesia resident; I'm Tim, the nurse." So when it comes to you, are you going to say, "I'm Doctor Gawande"? Or are you going to use your first name? The list actually helps to change the culture. Over and over again the feedback—especially from nurses and, often, the junior people on the team—has been that it's one of the most valuable steps. It raises the question "Is the hierarchy flattened here? Are we going to be a team?"

You wrote, "Maybe our idea of heroism needs updating." What did you mean?

Think of Sully Sullenberger, the pilot who landed that plane on the Hudson River. The way the public saw him was similar to how it wants to see doctors, and how doctors want to see themselves. The story the public had about him was that he was an unbelievable pilot, and that's what saved the plane. He was the hero. But he kept saying no, it was adherence to protocol and teamwork that allowed us to safely land the plane. Heroism in medicine ought to mean having the humility to recognize that we are more likely to fail on our own, and embracing teamwork to help us provide the best care.

But that works only if patients are willing to meet doctors halfway. Don't most patients want their doctor to be the old-fashioned kind of hero?

Not necessarily. When he was sick, Ted Kennedy wanted a heroic team, not a heroic individual. He had the neurosurgeons actually sit in his living room in Hyannis and argue with one another, and he conducted it like a seminar. "Well, Dr. X is arguing this—why wouldn't I do that?" he'd say. "Can you guys sort it out? I'm not the expert here. You guys are. Don't tell me, tell each other." As a result, he got wise care that allowed him to achieve a longer and more effective run at the end of his life than many of his doctors thought was possible. It's what we would all wish to have.

Isn't that what second opinions are for—to produce wise care?

The second opinion is a tremendously flawed institution. The idea is that you get two assessments and then pick the best doctor, the one you'll go with. But what you usually get is two different opinions, and then you don't know what to do. What you really want is for those two doctors to talk to each other.

GARDINER MORSE is a senior editor at *Harvard Business Review*.

Originally published in April 2010. Reprint R1004C

Fixing Health Care on the Front Lines

by Richard M.J. Bohmer

IN THE UNITED STATES and around the world, there have been plenty of proposals for curing what ails health care. All of them—new organizational forms, alternative payment systems, and free-market competition—aim to tackle a universal challenge: improving the quality of health care and reducing, or at least curbing, its soaring cost. But the reality is that regardless of what happens to the many experiments and reform efforts, including the one in Washington, the basic structure of the health care system in the United States and most other countries will remain in place for the foreseeable future. General hospitals, independent practices, and (in the United States) fee-for-service payment are not going to disappear anytime soon. The only realistic hope for substantially improving care delivery is for the old guard to launch a revolution from within. Existing players must redesign themselves.

What does "redesign" mean? Revamping core clinical processes and the organizational structures, management systems, and cultures supporting them so that health care providers excel at performing three discrete tasks simultaneously:

- Rigorously applying scientifically established best practices for diagnosing and treating diseases that are well understood

- Using a trial-and-error process to deal with conditions that are complicated or poorly understood

- Capturing and applying the knowledge generated by day-to-day care.

The vast majority of health care organizations throughout the world are not designed to excel at all three. In fact, they are not really "designed" at all. The elements of most general hospitals—buildings, technologies, clinical services—have accreted over time. And most hospitals don't determine how doctors work within their walls. Indeed, their role is to support physicians by assuring the quality and optimizing the availability of crucial resources for treating patients (nurses, beds, laboratories, X-ray facilities, and so on).

This is hardly surprising. The prevailing structures and processes reflect the nature of medical care before the explosion of medical knowledge over the past 30 years. They are legacies of the days when what was wrong with the patient and what to do about it were often opaque, disease incidence and progression were unpredictable, and each patient presented a unique set of challenges. Accordingly, diagnosis and treatment were left largely to the judgment of individual

Idea in Brief

In the United States and around the world, there have been plenty of proposals for curing what ails health care. All of them—new organizational forms, alternative payment systems, and free-market competition—aim to tackle a universal challenge: improving the quality of care and reducing, or at least curbing, its cost. But the reality is that regardless of what happens to the many experiments and reform efforts, including the one in Washington, the basic structure of the health care system in the United States and most other countries will remain in place for the foreseeable future. The only realistic hope for substantially improving care delivery is for the old guard to launch a revolution from within. Existing providers must redesign themselves. They must revamp core clinical processes and the organizational structures, management systems, and cultures supporting them so that they excel at performing three discrete tasks simultaneously: rigorously applying scientifically established best practices for diagnosing and treating diseases that are well understood; employing a trial-and-error process to deal with complicated or poorly understood conditions; and capturing and applying knowledge generated by day-to-day care. Some organizations—such as Intermountain Healthcare, the Cleveland Clinic, and Istituto Clinico Humanitas—have already redesigned themselves in ways that improve quality and lower costs. But no single dominant design exists; each organization has its own environment, structure, and history. More important than the specific designs are the four principles on which they are based: focus on the decisions, tasks, and workflows crucial to optimizing patient care; separate high- and low-variability care; reconfigure the supporting infrastructure and practices to match redesigned clinical processes; and design structure and processes to help organizations learn from their daily work.

physicians, who achieved the best possible outcomes by providing customized care. Medicine was a cottage industry of autonomous artisans. Hospitals were considered "the doctor's workshop."

Times have changed. Diagnosing and treating many diseases—diabetes, hypertension, and coronary artery disease, to name a few—are no longer a matter of educated guesswork. Scientific advances have vastly increased the volume and specificity of medical knowledge, which can be translated into standardized processes and programmed into computerized decision-support systems. And in some instances, tasks traditionally performed by physicians can be delegated to other personnel or even to patients.

The sad fact, though, is that science has far outstripped the ability of delivery organizations to apply it. Most are not configured to rapidly disseminate and use new knowledge. This helps explain why care known to be beneficial is not consistently administered, care of uncertain value is overprescribed, and avoidable harm abounds. By some estimates, it takes 10 to 20 years for a new practice to go from development to widespread adoption, and a recent RAND study found that in the United States the chance of receiving care that meets generally accepted standards is about 55%. Even though medical professionals since the middle of the nineteenth century have known that poor sanitation causes high rates of infection, simply getting care providers to routinely wash their hands remains a challenge.

Nor are delivery organizations very good at systematically learning how to tackle the toughest cases, which account for the majority of health costs—patients who have either multiple interacting conditions or diseases that are difficult to diagnose or for which there is no obvious, definitive treatment. The care of these patients is often spread among an array of medical subspecialists, physical and occupational therapists, dieticians, nurse practitioners, and social workers—all of whom work at different sites. As a result, no single entity is responsible for overseeing and learning from their collective work by analyzing data to discern patterns that reveal what is and is not working.

Modern health care organizations must be capable of simultaneously optimizing the execution of standardized processes for addressing the known and learning how to address the unknown—a tall order. A flaw in some of the proposals for fixing health care is the failure to address the complexity of patient care in which predictability and ambiguity exist side by side.

For example, some hospitals have applied principles of the Toyota Production System to perfect the technique for placing a central venous line. This has allowed them to reduce the associated infection rate to zero—a remarkable achievement—but it has not helped in the management of patients with multiple diseases whose condition is rapidly deteriorating. Similarly, retail clinics have increased access to and lowered the cost of care for patients with simple illnesses such as pinkeye and strep throat. But their response to people who come in with ambiguous problems is to refer them elsewhere. In short, no one approach is a panacea. Significant improvement in the overall quality and efficiency of health care will require redesigning delivery to integrate all such solutions.

Practically speaking, the main traditional players— established care-delivery networks, hospitals, and clinics—must lead the way in doing this. They are the only ones with the necessary size and scope. Some players have already begun reconfiguring themselves and making progress despite obstacles such as fee-for-service payment—a system that encourages the performance of procedures regardless of their impact on outcomes. Those that have attracted the most attention for their progress in eliminating waste and improving outcomes include Beth Israel Deaconess in Boston, Cincinnati Children's, Cleveland Clinic, Geisinger Health System in Pennsylvania, Intermountain Healthcare in Utah and Idaho, Istituto Clinico Humanitas near Milan, Kaiser Permanente in areas across the United States, and Virginia Mason in Seattle. These organizations understand that medical knowledge is now too voluminous to be stored in the heads of individual physicians and must instead be embedded in protocols and routines. In other words, they realize that curing disease has become an organizational responsibility. They consciously deploy their resources to achieve the best possible patient outcomes, collect and use data to relentlessly improve performance, and treat the daily practice of medicine as a source of insight and innovation.

But no single dominant design exists, which is not surprising given that each organization has its own environment, structure, and history. For example, Virginia Mason Medical Center is a single hospital whose physicians are salaried employees. Intermountain is a network of 25 hospitals with its own health plan whose doctors are a mix of salaried employees and independent practitioners. And the Mayo Clinic has a collaborative culture that dates back to the Mayo brothers' group practice in the late nineteenth century. An organizational design that is effective in one setting does not necessarily translate to another. More important than the specific designs are the four common principles on which they are based—the topic of the rest of this article.

Manage the Care

The first design principle is that the decisions, tasks, and workflows crucial to optimizing patient care must be the organization's primary focus. This represents a major change: Historically, delivery organizations have been structured to maximize the utilization of such resources as beds, tests, and procedure rooms. They have had little or no role in designing how specific illnesses were diagnosed and treated.

Although this model made sense when all care was judgment based and customized, it is a problem now that good outcomes depend on using well-developed evidence on the effectiveness of treatment to determine how care is provided and continuously learning from everyday practice. Applying evidence to practice requires standardization, not just of operational routines but also of the rules for making clinical decisions and executing tasks. Some hospitals have reduced infection rates by standardizing tasks such as the management of a patient on a ventilator. But others have gone further, specifying where possible the clinical decisions that precede tasks, such as whether the

Why Health Care Organizations Must Be Redesigned

THE EXPLOSION OF SCIENTIFIC KNOWLEDGE over the past 30 years has profoundly changed how medical professionals care for patients, but the structures and processes of most health care organizations are legacies of an earlier era.

Before

The nature of medicine before scientific advances...

Disease cause was unexplainable

Disease occurrence and progression were unpredictable

Treatment outcome was uncertain

Patients were heterogeneous and manifested diseases in different ways

. . . and how that shaped health care delivery

Who Fragmented and independent providers widely distributed in the community; diversified hospitals with the resources to cope with complex health problems

When At the patient's request

Where In specifically configured health care settings, such as a physician's office, a hospital ward, or a clinic

patient is a candidate for a test or therapy in the first place.

Intermountain provides an example of one approach to standardization. To the extent medical science allows, it specifies how a patient's health problems are diagnosed and treatments are selected and executed. In

What Customized diagnosis and treatment based on the individual physician's judgment

After

The nature of medicine after scientific advances...

Diagnoses are more accurate, treatment choices better specified, and treatments more reliable

Progression of disease and common complications and their precipitants are better characterized

Subgroups of patients with the same disease have been defined

... and the implications for how health care can be delivered

Who Professionals who are not necessarily doctors

When Before complications or exacerbations are manifest

Where Not necessarily during a face-to-face encounter between the patient and the care deliverer; in settings such as the patient's home, a fitness center, or a shopping mall

What Diagnosis and treatment based on highly specified protocols and decision rules; therapies targeting specific patient groups

---

contrast to the loosely worded clinical guidelines that have been common in health care, Intermountain's clinical processes are defined by protocols: detailed descriptions of the sequence of tasks and decisions that lead to the resolution of a patient's health problem. For instance, its community-acquired-pneumonia protocol lays out how the patient's history and results of physical examinations and laboratory tests should be used to make a diagnosis. These same data are used to ascertain the severity of the pneumonia using a well-validated calculation. This, in turn, determines where patients should be treated (in an outpatient clinic, on the ward, or in the intensive care unit) and the oral or intravenous antibiotic that is most likely to be effective.

At Intermountain, each protocol is drafted by a small team of paid clinical experts who review the scientific literature and Intermountain's own experience. The team defines each variable—symptom, physical observation, or laboratory result—and the expected timeline for the patient's diagnosis, treatment, and recovery. This information is translated into a sequence of yes/no check boxes and specific test and treatment choices laid out to mirror the order in which a doctor usually does his or her work. A larger team of general practitioners, nurses, and information-systems and administrative personnel then ensures that the protocol is workable in practice. Both teams are permanent; they track the scientific literature and the organization's experience, and make minor adjustments monthly and major revisions every two years.

Intermountain limits the work involved by creating protocols only for the roughly 70 conditions that make up more than 90% of its caseload. These are predominantly common adult diseases—such as diabetes, hypertension, coronary artery disease, and some cancers—for which there are established treatments supported by robust scientific evidence.

Corral Variability

Intermountain's protocols do not help diagnose and treat conditions that are complicated and poorly understood, or for which the right course of action is more ambiguous. More than a quarter of Americans over 65 suffer from four or more interacting diseases, and many have conditions for which there is no definitive treatment. As a result, the overall care they require is highly variable and cannot be standardized. Organizations that deal effectively with this challenge apply a second broad principle: High- and low-variability care must be separated.

Intermountain achieves this by allowing doctors to override standardized clinical processes in ambiguous situations. In other words, even though it standardizes as many treatments as possible, it expects—even en-courages—doctors to deviate from a protocol whenever they think doing so is in the patient's best interests. None of Intermountain's protocols is followed 100% of the time; the rate of deviation varies from one protocol to the next, depending in part on the inherent variation in the patient population with a given disease.

Another way to corral variability is to adopt the *hospital-within-a-hospital* (or *clinic-within-a-clinic*) model. This involves creating two units—one focused on uncomplicated cases and one on complicated cases. For example, at Duke University Medical System's clinic for treating congestive heart failure (CHF), one unit is staffed by nurse practitioners who apply standardized protocols to treat patients with uncomplicated CHF who are responding to treatment as expected. The other unit is staffed by cardiologists who use a wide array of tests and therapies and a customized process to address the needs of patients whose conditions are unstable, complex, or unusual in some way. This design allows the clinic to realize the benefits of operational focus—such as reliability, accuracy, and efficiency—while ensuring that no patient is turned away.

Istituto Clinico Humanitas uses a variant of this approach. Its campus comprises three distinct hospitals—elective, emergency, and rehabilitation—that are only a few hundred meters apart. Each has its own scope of work and focused operating system.

Organizations that employ the hospital-within-a-hospital model face three execution challenges. First, they need to ensure that all patients and caregivers have access to high-cost or scarce resources that must be shared, such as consultant senior doctors, nurses, and radiology services. Second, they must manage the interfaces between units so that patients can move quickly and smoothly between them as their needs demand. Finally, they must coordinate the flow of patients with complex or multiple illnesses among the specialized departments that contribute to their care.

Organizations can respond to these challenges in various ways. For example, Istituto Clinico Humanitas addresses the first by structuring its incentive system in a way that encourages doctors to consult in all three hospitals. Duke's CHF clinic relies on culture and process to address the second: It has embedded criteria in the protocols to initiate the transfer of a patient from one unit to another and has consciously created a collegial environment that fosters cooperation between nurse practitioners and cardiologists. To address the third, some organizations have created a coordinating function that shepherds patients through the various units providing their care.

In short, caring for patients with complex or poorly understood conditions demands sophisticated organizational designs. As specialized standalone services (such as clinics that treat simple illnesses or focus on a particular surgical procedure) proliferate, they need to be integrated into these designs. Yes, better information systems will help integrate them, but universal access to a patient's complete health record will not alone suffice. Without processes that coordinate care across organizational and professional boundaries, the fragmentation of care, already a headache for patients and their families and a source of waste, could worsen.

Reorganize Resources

The third principle is that when delivery organizations redesign clinical processes, they must also reconfigure the supporting infrastructure and practices. Unfortunately, many organizations don't match the resources—the mix of staff, the management structure, the measurement and incentive systems, the IT system, the physical layout of the clinic or ward, the rules for sharing resources, the technology for diagnosing and treating diseases, educational programs, and so on—with their redesigned processes. The result: Highly trained specialists continue to perform work that could be handed off to nurse practitioners. Protocols are not translated into easy-to-follow steps in the IT system. Performance measures and budgets are still focused largely on costs and volume of services rather than patient outcomes. And professionals who should operate in teams instead work in silos.

That is why diagnosing and determining how to treat a woman with a suspicious abnormality in her breast can still take weeks and require a multitude of separate appointments with a surgeon, a radiologist, and an oncologist. Some clinics have managed to collapse this to four hours by reorganizing these specialists into a colocated team that reviews the test results, decides whether a biopsy is necessary and performs it if so, analyzes the results, and, if cancer is confirmed, determines the treatment options.

In other industries, organizational structures and business processes are configured to support the core production process. But most hospitals use the same set of resources to offer services ranging from prevention and screening to the treatment of acute and chronic conditions to palliative end-of-life care. Resources are structured as separate job shops, and patients wend a circuitous path among them, often suffering delays along the way because of insufficient capacity.

Intermountain is an exception. It has reconfigured its resources to support its protocols. Here are some examples:

- The steps in its protocols have been embedded in its electronic-medical-record system. As a result, when a doctor determines that a patient has a moderate case of community-acquired pneumonia, a drop-down menu in the EMR offers a choice of two drug regimens.

- To train medical staff members and keep them up to date, educational materials and activities have been developed for each protocol.

- The teams responsible for developing protocols create measures that track compliance with and the impact of each one.

- Managers' compensation is determined in part by whether compliance with protocols meets predetermined goals established by Intermountain's board of directors. (Up to 25% of managers' compensation is tied to performance in six areas: clinical excellence, service excellence, physician engagement, operational effectiveness, employee engagement, and community stewardship.)

Health care organizations around the world are guided by the question "What care can we provide with the resources we have?" Whether the organization is a rural clinic in Rwanda treating AIDS and tuberculosis, a retail clinic at Wal-Mart handling minor ailments, or an academic medical center tackling the toughest, most complex cases, the question should be reversed: "What resources are required and how should they be configured for the care we need to provide?"

Some health care leaders will undoubtedly assume that their organizations cannot afford to adopt this mind-set, but it need not be expensive. Protocols and tracking measures are in the public domain. Data can be collected manually and analyzed inexpensively.

Learn from Everyday Care

The fourth principle is that the structure and processes of hospitals, clinics, and practices must be designed to help organizations systematically learn from their daily work. All too often, they are not. That's because of the traditional separation between the generation and application of medical knowledge: Basic scientists and clinical researchers create the knowledge, which is then taught to practicing doctors and nurses in the continuing education programs that they must take to maintain their licenses. And (in some countries) physicians' pay is tied to how well they incorporate this knowledge into their daily practice. In other words, knowledge flows one way—from research to practice.

In fact, valuable new knowledge about the nature of a disease, how to treat it, and how to organize the delivery of treatment is often generated by the daily practice of medicine. For example, two individuals—an obstetrician in Australia and a pediatrician in Germany—raised the alarm about thalidomide after observing in the late 1950s and early 1960s that patients in their practices who took the drug were giving birth to children with deformities. More recently, a group of cardiologists at the Mayo Clinic alerted the world that the diet drug combination Fen-Phen could cause pulmonary hypertension and heart-valve disease. And Kaiser Permanente's analysis of its own data helped show that Cox 2 inhibitors, a class of anti-inflammatory drugs, increase the risks of heart attack, thrombosis, and strokes. In all three cases, the drugs were withdrawn.

Some organizations, recognizing that their staff generates large and small insights and innovations that could have a tremendous impact on performance, develop routines for creating, capturing, and disseminating such knowledge. For example, when a doctor at Intermountain overrides a protocol, it is taken as a sign of the protocol's failure to meet the needs of a particular patient. The teams developing the protocols collect the overrides, analyze them for patterns in patient outcomes, and incorporate what they learn in their revisions.

In addition, a support unit at Intermountain, whose responsibilities include evaluating clinicians' innovative ideas, has the resources to conduct small-scale internal studies. For example, a critical-care doctor went to the unit to seek help in testing his hunch that if ward patients whose conditions were rapidly deteriorating were transferred to intensive care earlier, the mortality rate would be reduced. The unit helped him conduct internal studies that ultimately resulted in the development of criteria for transferring ward patients to the intensive care unit. The criteria included a respiratory rate of greater than 35 breaths per minute for more than 30 minutes, systolic blood pressure of less than 85 for more than 30 minutes, and a heart rate of less than 40 or more than 140 for any amount of time. Subsequent studies found that patients transferred to the ICU within four hours of meeting one of those criteria had a mortality rate one-fourth the rate of those transferred after more than four hours.

The Hard Work of Redesign

While the debates over health care reform continue to rage, a quiet revolution in health care delivery is under way. Organizations are applying the four design principles described in this article to improve patient outcomes. The lesson they offer is that no one solution can be imposed from on high: One size will not fit all. Each organization must base its design on the needs of the population it serves, the local regulatory environment, and the available resources.

The revolution, though, is still in its early days and will take years to have a widespread impact. That's because redesign is not just a matter of launching a few high-profile pilot programs; it involves an enormous amount of detailed work at each clinic, ward, and practice.

Intermountain has been developing its system for clinical performance management for several decades. Virginia Mason has spent eight years revamping hundreds of clinical and supporting business processes and the places where this work is done. Beth Israel Deaconess began developing its nationally acclaimed IT system in the 1960s. And the never-ending breakthroughs in medical knowledge mean that the work at these institutions will never be completed. It is only through such hard work that we will be able to remove waste in health care—the unnecessary bureaucracy, the duplicative or unnecessary tests, the therapies of minimal value, the inappropriate use of expensive venues such as emergency rooms, and so on—which is estimated to account for as much as 50% of health care spending.

Admittedly, there are some formidable internal obstacles to progress. Redesign requires doctors to work across silos and as members of a team, and to appreciate the value of designing and implementing care processes while knowing when and how to deviate from them. This runs counter to the training and experience of many physicians, who have been rewarded for their individual skill and actions. Many administrators do not know enough about the details of medical care to work with physicians in developing protocols and learning systems. And people who were appointed to boards of directors because of their community standing or fund-raising abilities often don't have the capabilities needed to govern clinical operations.

Then there are the well-known external obstacles, such as ossified government bureaucracies and, in the United States, fee-for-service reimbursement, which reduces the revenue of institutions and individuals that make quality improvements. Intermountain, for example, estimates that the improved outcomes from its community-acquired-pneumonia protocol resulted in lost revenue of more than $1 million annually because patients ultimately needed fewer services or could be cared for in lower-margin settings.

But these obstacles do not mean that change is impossible. Confronted with the trade-off between improving patient outcomes and maximizing short-term revenues, many organizations routinely choose the former.

Often absent from the debate about how to increase access and contain costs is an appreciation of the root cause of the upheaval in health care: the explosion in medical knowledge and technology and the resulting dramatic improvement in the quality and quantity of life. In any industry in which tacit knowledge becomes explicit, new production systems, organizational forms, and roles must be developed. Health care is no different. Government policies can aid in the transition, but the clinicians and managers who labor in the organizations where patients receive their care must do the hard work of redesign. Health care reform is as much a management as a policy challenge.

RICHARD M.J. BOHMER is a physician and a professor of management practice at Harvard Business School. He is the author of *Designing Care: Aligning the Nature and Management of Health Care* (Harvard Business Review Press, 2009).

Originally published in April 2010. Reprint R1004D

Fixing Health Care from the Inside, Today

by *Steven J. Spear*

LAST YEAR ON CHRISTMAS DAY, a 32-year-old Belgian woman celebrated the birth of a healthy daughter. Nothing remarkable about that, you might say, except that seven years prior, this same woman had been diagnosed with Hodgkin's lymphoma. Because doctors feared that chemotherapy would leave her infertile, they surgically removed, froze, and stored her ovaries. Once her treatment was concluded, with her cancer sufficiently in remission, they thawed the tissue and returned it to her abdomen, after which she was able to conceive and deliver.

Such medical miracles—improvements in fertility treatment, cancer cures, cardiac care, and AIDS management among them—are becoming so commonplace that we take them for granted. Yet, in the United States, the health care system often fails to deliver on the promise of the science it employs. Care is denied to many people, and what's provided can be worse than the disease. As many as 98,000 people die each year in U.S. hospitals from medical error, according to studies reviewed by the Institute of Medicine. Other studies indicate that nearly as many succumb to hospital-acquired infections.[1] The Centers for Disease Control and Prevention (CDC) estimates that for each person who dies from an error or infection, five to ten others suffer a nonfatal infection. With approximately 33.6 million hospitalizations in the United States each year, that means as many as 88 people out of every 1,000 will suffer injury or illness as a consequence of treatment, and perhaps six of them will die as a result. In other words, in the 15 to 20 minutes it might take you to read this article, five to seven patients will die owing to medical errors and infections acquired in U.S. hospitals and 85 to 113 will be hurt. Health care safety expert Lucian Leape compares the risk of entering an American hospital to that of parachuting off a building or a bridge.

How can this be in the country that leads the world in medical science? It's not that caregivers don't care. Quite the contrary: Health care professionals are typically intelligent, well-trained people who have chosen careers expressly to cure and comfort. For that reason, perhaps, many policy makers and management scholars believe that the problems with American health care are rooted in regulatory and market failures. They argue that institutions and processes mandated by law and custom are preventing demand for health care from matching efficiently to those most capable of providing it. In this view, the best treatment for what ails the U.S. health care

Idea in Brief

Every year, 98,000 people die in U.S. hospitals as a result of errors. And as many as 65 out of every 1,000 suffer injury or illness as a consequence of treatment.

In the nation that leads the world in medical science, what explains these alarming statistics? It's not that health care professionals lack intelligence, training, or compassion. Rather, operating under ambiguous, complex conditions, they work around problems to meet patients' needs. Problems' root causes go unexamined. Result? The same problems crop up repeatedly—sometimes with tragic consequences.

How can health care professionals radically improve patient care quality? Abandon work-arounds. Instead, apply the same operations-design principles that drive the renowned Toyota Production System (TPS): Use small, rapid experiments to uncover and solve problems as they occur. Clarify who's responsible for doing which procedures—and when and how. Foster a culture of continuous improvement by helping colleagues apply the experimental method to their own challenges.

By improving their work while they're actually doing it, health care practitioners can deliver extraordinary savings—in lives *and* dollars.

---

system is strengthening market mechanisms—rewarding doctors according to patient outcomes rather than the number of patients they treat, for instance; increasing access to information about health care providers' effectiveness to employers, individuals, and insurers; expanding consumer choice.

I won't dispute the benefits of these reforms. The efficiency of health care markets may indeed be gravely compromised by poor regulation, and economic incentives should reinforce health care providers' commitment to their patients. But I fear that the exclusive

Idea in Practice

To apply continual process improvement to health care:

Eradicate Ambiguities

Systematically identify and eliminate confusion over who does what—and when and how—in problematic work processes.

> *Example:* A hospital unit experienced difficulty completing blood work for presurgical patients. Nurses identified one cause: It wasn't always clear whether a patient's blood work had already been done. The solution? Put stickers on charts indicating the need for blood work. Another ambiguity involved who should draw blood: Busy nurses sometimes asked technicians to do it. To remove this confusion, the unit designated a staff member to draw all blood.

With eradication of such ambiguities, the number of surgery delays caused by incomplete blood work declined to zero, **saving $300 per minute** in operating-room staff time.

Score Big Gains Through Small Changes

Break big problems into manageable pieces. Generate a steady flow of changes that collectively deliver spectacular results.

> *Example:* A hospital wanted to reduce infections caused by insertions of intravenous catheters. Experts monitored all insertions and related activities. Each time they observed a problem (such as improper placement of lines) they immediately developed and tested a countermeasure. These included assigning responsibility for insertions only to specially trained practitioners and applying transparent dressings to facilitate assessment of wound sites.

pursuit of market-based solutions will cause professionals and policy makers to ignore huge opportunities for improving health care's quality, increasing its availability, and reducing its cost. What I'm talking about here are opportunities that will not require any legislation or market reconfiguration, that will need little or

Such changes reduced the number of patients suffering from infections from 37 to 6 in one year—and associated deaths from 19 to 1.

Conduct Simulations

Use trial runs of problematic processes to generate and test solutions.

> *Example:* One hospital pharmacy arranged a simulation to improve timely filling of medicine orders. A pharmacist and technician were paired in the pharmacy. Every three minutes (the average pace at which physicians submitted orders), they were handed one order to fill. Each time they couldn't fill an order within three minutes, they halted the simulation and asked themselves why. Problems included medications stored too far away, hard-to-read handwriting, and jammed label printers. By

developing solutions to these problems, the pharmacy reduced the incidence of delayed delivery of medications by 88%.

Institutionalize Change

To realize process improvement's full potential, ensure that senior health care leaders embrace it and help others master it.

> *Example:* One hospital's senior leadership team spent two weeks at Toyota factories observing their production system. The hospital subsequently trained all its 5,400 staffers in a care delivery process based on Toyota's operational principles. During 2002–2004, the number of patients contracting pneumonia in the hospital dropped from 34 to 4; and associated costs from $500,000 to $60,000.

no capital investment in most cases, and—perhaps most important—that can be started today and realized in the near term by the nurses, doctors, administrators, and technicians who are already at work.

The scale of the potential opportunities can be seen in the results of a number of projects I've been following over the past five years at various hospitals and clinics in Boston; Pittsburgh; Appleton, Wisconsin; Salt Lake City; Seattle; and elsewhere. Consider just one example. The CDC cites estimates indicating that bloodstream infections arising from the insertion of a central line (an intravenous catheter) affect up to 250,000 patients a year in the United States, killing some 15% or more. The CDC puts the cost of additional care per infection in the tens of thousands of dollars. Yet, two dozen Pittsburgh hospitals have succeeded in cutting the incidence of central-line infections by more than 50%; some, in fact, have reduced them by more than 90%. Rolled out throughout the U.S., these improvements alone would save thousands of lives and billions of dollars.

Other hospitals have dramatically lowered the incidence of infections arising from surgery and of pneumonia associated with ventilators. Still others have improved primary care, nursing care, medication administration, and a host of other clinical and nonclinical processes. All of these improvements have a direct impact on the safety, quality, efficiency, reliability, and timeliness of health care. Were the methods these organizations employ used more broadly, the results would be extraordinary. In fact, you could read an entire issue of HBR, even several, and during that time the number of fatalities would be close to zero. (See the exhibit "The health care opportunity.")

To understand how the improvements were achieved, it is necessary to appreciate why such a gap exists between the U.S. health care system's performance and

The health care opportunity

What if the improvements to medical care described in this article were adopted by every hospital in the United States? The following calculations estimate how many lives and how much money could be saved if actual rates (drawn from a number of conservative empirical studies) were cut in half—and if they were slashed by 90%.

Medical errors in U.S. hospitals		
Estimate of current annual level, nationwide	**Benefit if rate were cut 50%**	**Benefit if rate were cut 90%**
974,000 patients injured	487,000 patients avoiding injury	877,000 patients avoiding injury
44,000 to 98,000 deaths	22,000 to 49,000 lives saved	39,600 to 88,200 lives saved
$17 billion to $29 billion in costs	$8.5 billion to $14.5 billion saved	$15.3 billion to $26.1 billion saved

Preventable medication errors		
Estimate of current annual level, nationwide	**Benefit if mistakes were reduced by 50%**	**Benefit if mistakes were reduced by 90%**
185,000 patients injured	92,500 patients avoiding injury	166,500 patients avoiding injury
7,000 deaths	3,500 lives saved	6,300 lives saved
$2 billion in costs	$1 billion saved	$1.8 billion saved

(continued)

Central-line infections		
Estimate of current annual level, nationwide	Benefit if infections were reduced by 50%	Benefit if infections were reduced 90%
250,000 patients affected	125,000 patients avoiding infection	225,000 patients avoiding infection
30,000 to 62,500 deaths	15,000 to 31,250 lives saved	27,000 to 56,250 lives saved
$6.25 billion in costs	$3.13 billion saved	$5.63 billion saved

Sources: Unless otherwise noted, current figures are estimated from studies published in *To Err Is Human: Building a Safer Health System,* eds. Linda T. Kohn, Janet M. Corrigan, and Molla S. Donaldson (Institute of Medicine, 2000). Injuries from medical and medication errors are estimated from figures in Eric J. Thomas et al., "Incidence and Types of Adverse Events and Negligent Care in Utah and Colorado," *Medical Care* (Spring 2000). Central-line figures estimated from D.M. Kluger and D.G. Maki, "The Relative Risk of Intravascular Device–Related Bloodstream Infections in Adults," *Abstracts of the 39th Interscience Conference on Antimicrobial Agents and Chemotherapy* (American Society for Microbiology, 1999) cited in the CDC's August 9, 2002 weekly report of guidelines for prevention of central-line morbidity and mortality.

the skills and intentions of the people who work in it. The problem stems partly from the system's complexity, which creates many opportunities for ambiguity in terms of how an individual's work should be performed and how the work of many individuals should be successfully coordinated into an integrated whole. The Belgian woman's treatment, for instance, required a large number of oncologists, surgeons, obstetricians, pharmacists, and nurses both to perform well in their individual roles and to coordinate successfully with one another. Unless everyone is completely clear about the tasks that must be done, exactly who should be doing them, and just how they should be performed, the potential for error will always be high.

The problem also stems from the way health care workers react to ambiguities when they encounter them. Like people in many other industries, they tend to work around problems, meeting patients' immediate needs but not resolving the ambiguities themselves. As a result, people confront "the same problem, every day, for years" (as one nurse framed it for me) regularly manifested as inefficiencies and irritations—and, occasionally, as catastrophes.

But as industry leaders such as Toyota, Alcoa, Southwest Airlines, and Vanguard have demonstrated, it is possible to manage the contributions of dozens, hundreds, and even thousands of specialists in such a way that their collective effort not only is capable and reliable in the short term but also improves steadily in the longer term. These companies create and deliver far more value than their competitors, even though they serve the same customers, employ similar technologies, and use the same suppliers. Operating in vastly different industries, they have all achieved their superior positions by applying, consciously or not, a common approach to operations design and management.

As I have argued in previous articles in *Harvard Business Review,* what sets the operations of such companies apart is the way they tightly couple the process of doing work with the process of learning to do it better as it's being done. Operations are expressly designed to reveal problems as they occur. When they arise, no matter

Delivering Operational Excellence

FOUR BASIC ORGANIZATIONAL CAPABILITIES, if properly developed and nurtured, deliver the kind of operational excellence exhibited at Toyota and companies like it:

1. **Work is designed as a series of ongoing experiments that immediately reveal problems.** In order to drive out any ambiguity, employees in industry-leading companies spell out how work is expected to proceed in extraordinary detail, especially for highly complex and idiosyncratic processes. This increases the chance that the employees will succeed because it forces them to make their best understanding of a process explicit. If they don't succeed, spelling out what is expected increases the chance that problems will be detected earlier rather than later, since people will be surprised by the unexpected outcome. Such companies go even further by embedding tests into the work that show when what is actually happening is contrary to what was expected.

2. **Problems are addressed immediately through rapid experimentation.** When something does not go as expected, the problem is not worked around. Instead, it is addressed by those most affected by it. Its ramifications are contained and prevented from propagating and corrupting someone else's work. Causes are quickly investigated and countermeasures rapidly tested to prevent the problem from

---

how trivial they are, they are addressed quickly. If the solution to a particular problem generates new insights, these are deployed systemically. And managers constantly develop and encourage their subordinates' ability to design, improve, and deploy such improvements. (See the sidebar "Delivering Operational Excellence.")

This approach to operations can work wonders in health care, as the case studies in this article will show.

recurring. When those who first address a problem are flum-moxed, the problem is quickly escalated up the hierarchy so that broader perspectives and additional resources are brought to its resolution.

3. **Solutions are disseminated adaptively through collaborative experimentation.** When an effective countermeasure is developed, its use is not limited to where it has been discovered. But that doesn't mean the countermeasure is simply rolled out as a cookie-cutter solution. Rather, people build on local insights into reducing defects, improving safety, enhancing responsiveness, and increasing efficiency by solving problems with colleagues from other disciplines and areas so that the countermeasure, and the process by which it was developed, is made explicit, can be emulated, and can be critiqued.

4. **People at all levels of the organization are taught to become experimentalists.** Finally, managers at companies like Toyota don't pretend that the ability to design work carefully, improve processes, and transfer knowledge about those improvements develops automatically or easily. Coaching, mentoring, training, and assisting activities constantly cascade down to ever more junior workers, thereby building exceptionally adaptive and self-renewing organizations.

We will see examples of how health care managers and professionals have designed their operations to reveal ambiguities and to couple the execution of their work with its improvement, thus breaking free of the work-around culture. We will also see how health care managers have transformed themselves from rescuers arriving with ready-made solutions into problem solvers helping colleagues learn the experimental method.

I won't claim that moving to the new environment will be easy, given the complexities of the health care workplace. It will probably take some time, as well, because changes will have to be introduced gradually through pilot projects so as not to disrupt patient care. These changes will require serious commitment from health care managers and professionals at the highest levels. But the potential savings in lives alone—never mind the improved quality and increased access to health care that the dollar savings will make possible—are surely ample justification for attempting the voyage.

Let's begin by taking a closer look at what lies behind the health care tragedies we so often hear about.

Ambiguity and the Work-Around Culture

Typically, care in a hospital is organized around functions. Issuing medication is the responsibility of a pharmacist, administering anesthesia of an anesthetist, and so on. The trouble is, that system often lacks reliable mechanisms for integrating the individual elements into the coherent whole required for safe, effective care. The result is ambiguity over exactly who is responsible for exactly what, when, and how. Eventually a breakdown occurs—the wrong drug is delivered or a patient is left unattended. Then, doctors and nurses improvise. They rush orders through for the right drugs, urge colleagues to find available room for patients, or hunt down critical test results. Unfortunately, once the immediate symptom is addressed, everyone moves on without analyzing and fixing what went wrong in the first place. Inevitably, the problem recurs, too often with fatal consequences.

Consider the story of Mrs. Grant, which comes to us from a 2002 article by David W. Bates in the *Annals of Internal Medicine*. A 68-year-old woman Bates called Mrs. Grant (all individuals' names in this article are likewise pseudonyms) had been recovering well from elective cardiac surgery when, all of a sudden, she began to suffer seizures. Her blood was drawn for testing, and she was rushed for a CT scan, which revealed no hemorrhage, mass, or other obvious cause. When she was returned to her room, caregivers saw from her blood test results that she was suffering from acute hypoglycemia, and they tried unsuccessfully to raise her blood sugar level. She quickly fell into a coma, and after seven weeks her family withdrew life support.

How could that have happened? A subsequent investigation revealed that at 6:45 on the morning of the incident, a nurse had responded to an alarm indicating that an arterial line had been blocked by a blood clot, and he had meant to flush the line with an anticoagulant, heparin. There was, however, no evidence that any heparin had been administered. What investigators did find was a used vial of insulin on the medication cart outside Mrs. Grant's room, even though she had no condition for which insulin would be needed. Investigators concluded that the nurse had administered insulin instead of heparin and that this error had killed the patient. In retrospect, the mistake was understandable. Insulin and heparin (both colorless fluids) were stored in vials of similar size and shape, with labels that were hard to read, and they were located next to each other on the cart.

Mrs. Grant's tragedy illustrates both the ambiguity that typifies many health care environments and the drawbacks of a work-around culture. The drugs were packaged, labeled, and stored the way they were because the people responsible for doing so did not understand how their decisions about such specifics might cause problems for the nurses administering the drugs. As a consequence, safety depended heavily on nursing staff vigilance. Given how fragmented and hurried nursing work is, that was asking a lot at the best of times. In Mrs. Grant's case, the timing of the mistake may have increased its likelihood, as the insulin was administered early in the morning, when the nurse might not have been fully alert, in a room that may have been dimly lit.

Mrs. Grant's nurse was certainly not the first in this hospital to have confused insulin with heparin. In fact, Bates (et al.) in a 1995 study found that for every death due to medication error there were ten injuries that weren't fatal and 100 instances where harm was averted. In other words, most of the time people make a mistake, they prevent it from harming the patient, mainly by catching themselves in time and replacing the wrong drug with the right one. Because they usually correct themselves quickly, almost reflexively, they seldom draw attention to the error. It is only after a patient dies or suffers a serious injury that the type of mistake and the factors contributing to it are subject to serious scrutiny.

Not all medical errors are the result of individuals failing in the face of challenges presented by confusing situations. Take the case, investigated by the Centers for Medicare & Medicaid Services, of a five-year-old boy who had electrical sensors surgically implanted in his brain to treat his epilepsy. Six hours after the operation, seizures began to rack the boy's entire body; anticonvulsant medication needed to be administered immediately. Yet even though several neurosurgeons, neurologists, and staff members from the medical intensive care unit (MICU) were either in the room, on call nearby, or at the end of a telephone, too little medication was administered too late. The boy suffered a heart attack 90 minutes into the seizures and died two days later.

When the investigators asked the doctors and nurses involved how the boy could have died surrounded by so many skilled professionals, they all explained that they had assumed at the time that someone else was responsible for administering the drugs. The MICU staff thought that the neurologists were in charge. The neurosurgery staff thought the MICU and neurologists were responsible. The neurologists thought the other two services had the lead. Those on the phone deferred to those at the patient's bedside.

Each of the professionals had probably been involved in hundreds of similarly ambiguous transfers of care. In those cases, however, either the patient didn't suffer an unexpected crisis or one of the parties involved stepped in and took a decisive lead. Unfortunately, the success of those sometimes heroic work-arounds concealed the ambiguity that made them necessary in the first place.

Nailing the Ambiguities

What can hospitals and clinics do to prevent such tragedies? The experience of the presurgery nursing unit at Western Pennsylvania Hospital ("West Penn") in Pittsburgh shows how organizations can make the transition from an ambiguous environment filled with work-arounds to one in which problems become immediately apparent and are dealt with as they occur.

On a typical day, the hospital's presurgical nursing unit prepared some 42 patients for scheduled surgery. On arrival, a patient registered with a unit secretary, who entered the person into the system. Then a nurse took the patient's medical history and conducted a physical examination. A critical part of this prepping job was drawing blood for testing, which provided essential information for the surgical team. Sometimes, the examining nurse drew the blood; other times, she asked a technician to do it; still other times, if something intruded on the nurse's attention, no one would do it. The result of this catch-as-catch-can procedure was that, on average, the blood work for one in six patients failed to be completed before the patient was ready to go to the operating room. This was costly in a number of ways. A delay in getting a patient to the OR meant idling OR staff, at an estimated cost of $300 per minute. It also meant delaying care—even canceling it, in some instances—for a patient who had been fasting and was anxious about the procedure.

When the unit reviewed the steps used in drawing blood, it uncovered, and then eliminated, a series of ambiguities in the process in a systematic way. First, though it was clear that blood needed to be drawn for every patient, it was often not clear to the nursing staff whether the procedure had already been done. To eliminate this confusion, the unit introduced visual indicators to identify which patients still needed the procedure and which did not. These indicators included stickers on charts and signs on the ends of beds, both of which could be deployed easily during the presurgical preparation.

But even when it was clear which patients needed blood drawn, it was not clear who should do it. The nurse? A technician? To deal with this second ambiguity, the unit designated a particular staff member, whom we'll call Mary, to be the sole person to draw blood from every patient. Mary's appointment had positive results: The number of prepped patients missing blood test results fell sharply. Nonetheless, some patients were still ready for surgery before their tests were complete.

It turned out that even if Mary knew which patients needed their blood drawn, she didn't always know soon enough to get results back in time for their surgery. To give the lab the most time to process the sample, nurses agreed that blood should be drawn as soon as a patient was registered.

This improvement also reduced, but did not eliminate, the problem. In investigating further incidents, the nursing staff found yet another degree of ambiguity. Although Mary now knew she was responsible for drawing blood once the patients were registered, she didn't always know when the registration had been completed. There was no clear signal that Mary should begin her work. To resolve this, Mary and the unit's registration secretary specified a simple, reliable, and unambiguous visual signal—a card would be placed on a rack. If no cards were on the rack, no samples needed to be taken. If one card was on the rack, a patient had been registered and was ready to have a sample taken. Two or more cards beginning to pile up on the rack was a clear sign that Mary was taking samples at a rate slower than patients were arriving.

Despite all these improvements, a few patients were still turning up for the OR without their blood work. Mary and her colleagues took another look at their process. It was clear which patients needed to have blood drawn, who was responsible for drawing the blood, and when Mary needed to draw it. What still wasn't clear was where the procedure should take place. To eliminate this final ambiguity, the unit converted a small closet into a room for drawing blood. Stored items were removed, the walls were painted, lighting was installed, supplies were stocked, and a comfortable chair was provided for patients. With this final change, the number of patients ready for the OR without blood work declined to—and stayed at— zero.

In addition to the blood-drawing initiative, Mary's unit conducted a number of similar projects to improve the reliability of work through high-speed, iterative trials. One such effort was targeted at improving patient comfort and dignity. In the past, the unit had moved patients as far along in presurgical preparation as possible to ensure that surgeons were never kept waiting. This included getting patients to change into those uncomfortable, overly revealing hospital gowns well ahead of time, which meant that they had to wait around in public for an average of 25 minutes before being given a bed.

A team in the unit spent half a day piloting a number of innovations to allow patients to delay changing until a bed was free. Team members tested out and then established signals to indicate which bed was to be available for whom, when. A changing area was created, equipped with various signs and directions designed to ensure that patients wouldn't get lost or misplace their personal effects. Before choosing the area, the team tested different rooms and screen configurations to see how well they provided privacy and made it easy to change clothes. The changes made a considerable difference. The number of patients waiting in public in their gowns at any one time fell from as many as seven to zero. Now they could wait in their street clothes with family members until beds were ready.

West Penn's improvements didn't happen because frontline workers all of a sudden started avoiding work-arounds and instead paused to construct reliable countermeasures. Much of the credit for the successes can be attributed to the problem-solving support provided by the unit's clinical coordinator, Karen, whose role was redefined in the course of the projects.

Previously, she had been the person of last resort when unit staffers couldn't construct their own work-arounds. If they couldn't get some needed paperwork, she got it; if lab tests were missing, she chased them down. Karen's new responsibilities were very different. Staffers brought all problems, including those they could work around themselves, to her attention one by one, as they occurred, rather than after the fact (if at all) in a group. Once alerted to a problem, Karen worked with whoever had raised it to investigate the causes, develop a solution, and test and validate the changes. These were not ad hoc solutions—like putting pressure on the pharmacy to rush a particular order—but rather basic changes in the design of work that were meant to entirely prevent the problem from recurring.

In the highest-performing organizations, all workers—not just those on the front line—need to be coached to learn how to reduce ambiguity systematically and how to continually improve processes through quick, iterative experiments. Thus, to help find her way into the new approach, Karen had a mentor—Alex—who worked with her several days a week. A former hospital administrator, Alex had been trained in the principles of the Toyota Production System. Alex's role was not to teach Karen how to apply to the hospital environment the widely used tools of TPS, such as andon cords or kanban cards, but rather to teach her how to develop analogous

Eliminating ambiguity and work-arounds

In the moment, it may seem that when you are faced with a problem, the most effective thing to do is work around it as quickly as possible, particularly when lives are in the balance. But see how much time was saved—and how much patient care improved—when people at Western Pennsylvania Hospital stopped working around problems, and ambiguities in work processes were systematically eliminated through a series of rapid experiments facilitated by a manager.

Metric	The ambiguous, work-around system	The rapid-experiment approach
Time between signing in and starting registration:	Up to 2 hours	0
Time spent registering patients:	12 minutes to 1 hour	3 minutes
Time spent assembling patients' charts:	9 hours each day	2¼ hours
Number of charts with unstamped pages:	35	less than 1
Nurses' time wasted as a result, each day:	70 minutes	negligible
Number of gowned patients waiting on chairs in hallway:	4 to 7 at any given time	0
Time spent waiting in gowns in public:	25 minutes, average	0
Number of patients whose lab results are incomplete:	7 out of 42	0
Availability of supplies:	Some unavailable; others overstocked but past expiration	All available when, where, and in the quantity required
Number of unnecessary blood bank reports issued:	10 to 11 per day	0

problem-solving techniques and tools that took into account the idiosyncrasies of her unit.

In the year after Karen's role was redefined, her unit identified and tackled 54 separate problems—about one a week. These varied in scope, impact, and time involved, but each followed the approach I've just described. As the table "Eliminating ambiguity and work-arounds" shows, a systematic approach to eliminating problems need not take any more time than a temporary work-around.

Big Gains Through Small Changes

The changes I've described at West Penn were individually small, but taken together they led to marked improvement in the presurgical unit's performance. That's also characteristic of change at Toyota: People don't typically go in for big, dramatic cure-alls. Instead, they break big problems into smaller, tractable pieces and generate a steady rush of iterative changes that collectively deliver spectacular results. This determination to sweat the small stuff underlies the remarkable reduction in central line–associated bloodstream (CLAB) infections achieved by the hospitals participating in the Pittsburgh Regional Healthcare Initiative (PRHI).

Used to speed the delivery of medication, central lines are intravenous catheters placed in the blood vessels leading to the heart. Infections arising from this procedure exact a terrible cost. The figures that I cited at the top of this article—250,000 patients suffering central-line infection in U.S. hospitals, with some 15%

Radically reducing infection

In less than three years, using techniques adapted from the Toyota Production System, the Pittsburgh Regional Healthcare Initiative slashed the number of reported central line-associated bloodstream (CLAB) infections by more than 50%. The rate per 1,000 line days (the measure the hospitals use) plummeted from 4.2 to 1.9.

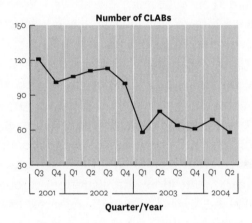

Number of CLABs

Quarter/Year

or more deaths—are only averages. The mortality rate at just one PRHI member, LifeCare Hospitals of Pittsburgh, was a staggering 40%, and the cost for each case was anywhere between $25,000 and $80,000.

The CDC has developed guidelines for the placement and maintenance of central lines. But as the PRHI professionals realized, the guidelines are generic to all hospitals and do not take into account the idiosyncratic factors of patient, place, and worker that are the root causes of individual infections. To improve their central-line processes, therefore, the PRHI hospitals decided to identify all the potential sources of central-line infection and all the local variations. As a result, the countermeasures these hospitals generated were tailored to the caseload, staffing, and special requirements of individual institutions and units. Nevertheless, the hospitals developed their countermeasures in the same way that Mary, Karen, and their colleagues did at West Penn. They responded swiftly to individual problems, testing a variety of possible solutions quickly, and those more senior took on the responsibility of enabling those more junior to succeed in the design and improvement of the work.

At Monongahela Valley Hospital, for example, a team of infection control experts documented every line placement to identify all variations and their shortcomings. They carefully monitored all line insertions, dressing changes, medication administrations through the line, and blood draws for even the minutest breaks in technique and sterility. Each time the team observed a problem with the process, it would immediately develop and test some kind of countermeasure.

Like the innovations developed at West Penn, the countermeasures these hospitals developed were all aimed at removing ambiguity and increasing specificity in the same way—specifically, at four levels of system design: system output, responsibility, connection, and method. As they did at West Penn, the changes at the PRHI hospitals were designed to make crystal clear

- who was to get what procedure (output),

- who was to do which aspect of placing and maintaining the lines (responsibility),

- exactly what signals would be used to trigger the work (connection), and

- precisely how each step in the process would be carried out (method).

For instance, several hospitals required that the central lines in all new admissions be replaced, since the histories of those lines were not known, thus simplifying output. To ensure that lines were properly placed, some units assigned responsibility only to those who had been specifically trained in each hospital's most up-to-date techniques (while expanding the size of that group through additional training).

In terms of connections, visual signals, such as stickers, were added to patients' charts and beds to trigger the removal of catheters sooner rather than later. Other such signals were used to indicate when a catheter should be moved from a place on the body known to have a high risk of infection to a lower-risk area and to otherwise clarify when lines had to be maintained or replaced. Transparent dressings were used to make it easier to tell whether a wound site was healthy or not.

As for methods, changes were made in disinfectant materials and techniques, and the kits in which line maintenance supplies came were repeatedly modified. (One alteration was to pack gloves on the top of the kit so that people would not contaminate other components in getting at the gloves.) Tests were made of various sized surgical drapes to determine which were not so small as to be ineffective or so big that they were knocked out of place when patients moved.

Combining Countermeasures Has a Big Effect

IN THEIR QUEST TO ELIMINATE central line–associated bloodstream (CLAB) infections, the hospitals in the Pittsburgh Regional Healthcare Initiative instituted a plethora of small process enhancements that together added up to dramatic improvement.

LifeCare Hospitals
Countermeasure

- Avoid femoral lines because of increased infection risk.

- Change type of disinfectant.

- Use transparent dressings to improve visibility of wound to caregivers and reduce the need for physical manipulation as part of inspection.

- Call out every hand-washing lapse.

- Have nurses ask doctors each day if catheters can be removed or placed in lower-risk sites.

- Change lines for all new admissions, since history of current line is not known.

- Report every infection to the CEO every day, and investigate each one immediately.

Result

87% reduction in CLAB infections even as the number of lines placed rose by 9.75%.

Monongahela Valley Hospital
Countermeasure

- Require that kits always be complete so that practitioners can always don full protective garb.

- Require the lab to call the moment a positive culture is identified; initiate a root cause analysis immediately.

- Avoid femoral lines.

Result

Since 2002, zero infections in medical intensive care unit (MICU), 1 in cardiac care unit (CCU). (National average is 5 infections per 1,000 line days.) Zero urinary tract infections and zero ventilator-associated pneumonias in MICU and CCU for 6 months.

UPMC Health System
Countermeasure

- Ensure hand-washing compliance.

- Improve barrier kits and use them in a consistent manner.

- Allow medical residents to place lines only with supervision until they all are formally trained.

Result

One MICU went without a CLAB infection for several months. Systemwide rate cut to 1.2 infections per 1,000 line days.

Allegheny General Hospital
Countermeasure

- Investigate each infection as it's discovered.

- Remove all femoral lines within 24 hours.

- Prohibit rewiring of dysfunctional lines.

- Remove all catheters for transferred patients.

- Use biopatch dressings for lines that are expected to be in place for two weeks or more.

Result

Infections down from 37 in 2003 to 6 in 2004; deaths down from 19 to 1 in the same period. Direct cost reduction of $1.4 million.

The results of the initiative were impressive. At Allegheny General Hospital alone, the number of patients suffering from central-line infections declined from 37 in one year to six in the following year, and associated deaths fell from 19 to one. (To see the cumulative effect, see the sidebar "Combining Countermeasures Has a Big Effect.")

Simulation and Experiment

On any given day, Toyota employees engaged in design and production will be conducting some kind of simulation or experiment with workers and managers, repeatedly figuring out how to test ideas as quickly and inexpensively as possible. People bolt what they would otherwise weld, tape what they would otherwise bolt, and just hold in place what they would otherwise tape. The objective is to compress the time between when an idea is formulated and when it is tested.

The pharmacy at the University of Pittsburgh Medical Center (UPMC) South Side hospital used this approach in identifying and solving problems with its medication delivery process. The pharmacy was supposed to make timely deliveries of medication throughout the hospital so that nurses could administer drugs to their patients according to the appropriate schedule. But when nurses went to get the medications, they often found that what they needed was missing. This triggered work-arounds. Nurses would interrupt their work to call the pharmacy, requiring pharmacy staff to stop what they were doing to track down orders:

Had they been received? Had they been entered? Had they been prepared? Had they been delivered? Where was the missing medication? How quickly could it be rushed to the person needing it? Tracking down a missing medication, with all the attendant interruptions, could consume hours of nurse, pharmacist, and technician time.

The problem, the pharmacy realized, was that medication administration was done in batches. Physicians would make rounds early in the morning—before office hours or surgery—and follow up throughout the day. As patients' conditions changed, doctors would write further orders for medication, which would be collected and delivered periodically to the pharmacy. There, pharmacists would enter the orders into the computer system, their expertise allowing them to identify potential problems with dosage, interactions, allergies, and the like. Orders would accumulate in the computer system throughout the day and then be printed out for all patients in the late afternoon. The next day, the pharmacy staff would begin filling these orders, assembling the proper mix and volume for each patient. This work would be completed in the early afternoon, at which point, a delivery technician would bring the completed orders to the nursing units. In view of the 12 to 24 hours that elapsed between the writing and the filling of an order, it was quite likely that medication needs would change, triggering work-arounds to get patients the right medicines, as well as a lot of unnecessary work restocking the old orders and making sure that patients were not billed for drugs they no longer needed.

The temptation in these situations is to brainstorm your way to an answer, with everyone proposing solutions drawn from his or her personal experience. But this was not the approach chosen here. As a first step in determining how to fix the medication preparation process, the pharmacy staff sat down as a group to determine what demands the nursing units were actually placing on the pharmacy. They counted out the previous day's orders, divided that by the number of hours the pharmacy operated, and concluded that if the pharmacy were operating at the pace at which medication was being consumed, it would have to produce and deliver one order every three minutes. This gave them a concrete goal—instead of asking what changes they needed to make the process "better," they asked what specifics prevented them from performing perfectly.

To answer that question, they set up a simulation. One pharmacist and one technician were lined up in the pharmacy, and every three minutes they were handed one order, which they tried to fill. This being an experiment, the staff used the previous day's orders, not that day's, and they delivered the medication into a cardboard box rather than having a delivery technician bring the medication all the way to the nursing unit. A stopwatch was started, a colleague handed the pair the first order, and they filled it. Three minutes later, the pharmacist and technician were handed a second order, which they filled. They were handed a third order, but before they could complete the work of finding the medication in inventory, taking out the right sized dose, labeling it, checking it, and bagging it, the three-minute interval had elapsed, and they were handed the fourth order.

At this point, they halted the experiment and asked themselves: "Why couldn't we fill the third order?" This question was critical, and semantics mattered. Asking "Why *didn't* you do your work?" elicits a very different response, typically a defensive explanation about how hardworking someone is, how he isn't trying to fail, and so on. Asking why one *couldn't* fill the order elicits a specific impediment, such as some ingredient being stored too far away or someone's handwriting being too hard to read.

In this case, the pair realized that they couldn't fill the order because the medication they were seeking couldn't be found, and by the time they were done searching for it, their time was up. That very specific reason was recorded—"medicine X was in an uncertain location"—and the experiment resumed. A new order was handed to the team, and it was filled. Three minutes passed. Another order, another successful delivery to the cardboard box. Three more minutes. Another order—and another problem. When one of them tried to take a label off the printer, it jammed, delaying the process and preventing the team from keeping pace— another specific problem to be solved. The process of trying to fill one order every three minutes continued throughout the morning, and by the lunch break the experimenters had dozens of very specific answers to why the pharmacy couldn't fill each order in time.

Some of the problems were easy to fix, such as storing drugs according to how frequently they were used rather than alphabetically. Others were more complicated, such as changing the timing at which drugs left the pharmacy, the delivery route technicians took through the hospital, and the way orders were placed with distributors. But simple or complex, the changes had a big cumulative impact. The pharmacy was ultimately never able to process and deliver each order individually, largely because the doctors writing the orders tended to do so in batches as they made their rounds, and delivery techs could not run so many individual orders to their various destinations at the same time. But the pharmacy did manage to process batches of medication once every two hours instead of once every 24 hours. As a result, the incidence of missing medications in the wards dropped 88%.

The savings in terms of pharmacy time and medication management were equally impressive. Time spent searching for medication fell by 60% and stock-outs fell by 85%—with no investment in technology. Overall medication inventory was reduced, and medication costs dropped because drugs were less likely to be lost, spoiled, or wasted. Under the old system, for instance, IV medications were delivered as much as 48 hours *before* they were actually needed. That was problematic because many IV medications had to be refrigerated or otherwise kept in a controlled fashion, taking up valuable storage space in nursing units. What's more, a patient's condition often changed before the IV was to be administered, so more than 30% of IV medications were returned to the pharmacy. Since some medications spoil quickly once mixed with a saline solution, the pharmacy staff was often obliged to throw out the returns. Under the new process, IV medications were prepared and delivered shortly before being needed, significantly reducing both waste and demands on storage in the wards.

What happened after the UPMC South Side experiment was almost more interesting than the experiment itself. When OR support staffers at UPMC Shadyside hospital learned of the improvements at South Side, they tried to apply the same tools and practices. But they soon discovered that the South Side solutions were inappropriate because of differences in the two organizations' work. So the Shadyside people visited South Side and walked through the simulation process I've just described. As they did so, they came to see that what they needed to do was master the problem-solving *process* rather than the problem-specific *solutions*. Accordingly, they set up a similar experiment at their own site, uncovered different problems, and found different solutions.

The Model Line Approach

When organizations first analyze their problems, they are inevitably tempted to roll out their solutions throughout the organization by installing a common set of tools and procedures broadly and quickly. But there are a couple of difficulties with that approach.

First, as Shadyside discovered, the solutions from one situation may not apply in another. Second, the most effective changes—at West Penn, South Side, and elsewhere—are small ones, generated by rapid experiments. Draw too big a group into the initial deployment, and the experiments become unwieldy, requiring too many people to change too much of their work at the same time. After all, even a small nursing unit includes several nurses in each day, evening, and night shift, as well as fill-ins for weekends, vacations, and the like and dozens of doctors who can admit patients to the unit. Finally, what sets companies like Toyota apart is not their portfolio of existing solutions but their ability to generate new ones repeatedly. One way to hone that ability is through the "model line" concept—creating, essentially, a model of the production line, a small incubator within the larger organization in which people can develop and practice the ability to design and improve work through experiments, and managers can rehearse their roles in facilitating this ongoing problem-solving and improvement process.

Shadyside used the model line approach with great success in its efforts to raise several aspects of the quality of its care. Rather than swamp the staff with a large initiative, the hospital began with a few beds within a single nursing unit and at first addressed just one of the many problems affecting nurses' ability to care for patients.

Like many hospitals, Shadyside found that its nurses spent a disproportionate amount of time nursing not the patients but the system—tracking down materials, services, and information. One consistent aggravation was with patient-controlled anesthesia (PCA) pumps. Nurses needed access keys to adjust dosages, but for security reasons the pharmacy had assigned the unit only a few keys, which were often hard to find. So, as a work-around, the nurses would go looking for the most recent user. Nurses in each shift searched for keys to the narcotics cabinet on average 23 times, wasting 49 minutes a shift and delaying pain relief to patients.

In discussing the problem, the nurses quickly realized that the limited number of keys was the issue. A nurse needing a key would check it out with the unit secretary but often fail to return it when rushing to meet another patient's needs. The solution piloted was to have a numbered key available for every nurse, which would be signed out at the beginning of the shift and signed back in only when the nurse left the unit or ended his or her shift. In this way, the pharmacy's need to control drug access was satisfied without inconveniencing the nurses. The time spent searching for keys was reduced to almost zero, and the practice was subsequently deployed throughout the hospital, saving an estimated 2,900 nurse-hours each year.

The nurses in the unit then applied their problem-solving approach to another issue: patient falls. An estimated 2% to 4% of patients fall during their hospitalization in the United States every year (which translates into 670,000 to 1.3 million individuals) and 2% to 6% of those spills (13,000 to 78,000) lead to injury. At Shadyside, the average was one fall every 12 hours. When the nurses looked into the problem, they realized that they hadn't made it clear who was at risk of falling. What's more, patient escorts were not trained in helping patients in and out of beds or on and off gurneys. That meant escorts would leave patients to find a trained nurse. Bit by bit, the unit's nurses introduced changes, in much the same way the West Penn team did. When they first arrived at the unit, patients were rated at risk or not. Escorts were taught how to safely transfer patients so that they wouldn't have to leave patients unattended. Danger areas were clearly marked (for instance, labels that said, "Don't leave me alone!" were placed by bedside toilets). Nurses and nurse assistants built into their work the regular inquiry, "Do you need to use the bathroom?" so patients wouldn't try to get out of bed on their own. Sensors were placed on beds to indicate if a patient was trying to get out of bed unassisted. And patients who needed but arrived without walkers or canes were lent the equipment they needed. After the changes were introduced, the number of falls declined dramatically—at one point, the unit went 95 days without one.

The nurses' success with PCAs and falls was not lost on the staff from the dietary department serving the same unit. The problem facing the dietitians was that they could not tell how well patients adhered to the dietary regimens appropriate for their medical conditions. Patients on restricted diets would cheat ("I can't eat this tasteless mess: Honey, can you grab me a burger, fries, and shake from the cafeteria downstairs?"). Even if patients did stick to the regimen in the hospital, they often stopped when they left, potentially compromising their recovery.

After discussing the problem-solving approach with the nurses, the dietitians realized that they could use patient meals as a way to identify precisely which patients would need further education. Rather than restrict choices, they decided to let the patients in the unit pick from the hospital's entire menu—a counterintuitive approach if your objective is to control what patients eat but not if your objective is to teach patients how to select wisely and discover when your efforts have not succeeded. Allowing patients to choose from the whole menu was coupled with counseling from dietary and nursing staff about what foods should be chosen or avoided. Menu selections were coded—with a "healthy heart" sticker, for example, to indicate low-fat options—to make it clear which choices were appropriate for the various restricted diets. Then, after patients ordered food, dietitians would compare the orders with the instructions in the patients' charts. Inappropriate picks—say, a cardiac patient ordering a high-cholesterol meal—would be treated as problems, and dietary and nursing staff would visit every problem patient before the meal was even served to provide nutritional instruction. If, after repeated counseling, patients continued to make choices contrary to recommendations, dietary and nursing staff would inform their doctors, who could modify their postdischarge medication orders appropriately, changing, for example, the type or dosage of blood pressure medication for a patient who wouldn't cut his sodium intake.

Conemaugh Health System in west central Pennsylvania used an interesting variant of the model line approach to reveal problems that spanned the boundaries of individual units and departments. To find out what was falling between the cracks, the hospital tracked the treatment of certain patients all the way from admission to discharge.

One patient had come for a cardiac catheterization following symptoms that included chest discomfort. Testing revealed no blockage, and the patient was scheduled for discharge. From the patient's perspective, this was a happy outcome, but from the hospital's perspective, the findings were sobering: The team dealing with the patient documented that fully 27 distinct and potentially dangerous problems had occurred. While none actually compromised the care given to this particular patient, team members didn't want to leave the ambiguities that caused the problems in place to be worked around again, so they worked with the pharmacy, the lab, and other departments to resolve them.

Institutionalizing Change

If one asks the question, Can the Toyota Production System be applied in health care? the quick answer is yes. The experiments I've just described all demonstrate that possibility. But to realize the full potential of TPS, senior health care leaders—hospital CEOs, presidents, chiefs of staff, vice presidents for patient care, medical directors, unit directors, and the like—will need to do more than provide support for pilot projects. They will need to embrace and embody TPS in their own work. An example from the Virginia Mason Medical Center (VMMC) illustrates what it means for managers to try to master this new approach.

VMMC is a 300-bed, Seattle-based teaching hospital with 5,400 employees and 400 physicians who admit some 16,000 patients a year and serve more than a million outpatients at ten sites. VMMC's management first became interested in TPS in 2001, after executives from local businesses described the dramatic improvements they had achieved in quality, customer satisfaction, safety, staff satisfaction, and, not least, profitability. At the time, VMMC was in sorry straits. The hospital was struggling to retain its best people, and issues of quality, safety, and morale were on everyone's mind.

VMMC started by piloting a few projects along the lines I've described in previous sections. But managers didn't really understand the potential of establishing a continuously self-improving organization until the hospital's chairman and its president, together with its professional and physician executives, went in 2002 on a two-week visit to Toyota factories, during which they all took part in an improvement project at a Toyota affiliate. Impressed by the knowledge that it was possible to establish such an organization, VMMC formally adopted TPS as a model for its management system and began to train all of its staffers in its philosophy, principles, and tools. That included a public commitment to retain all full-time employees so that people would not feel that they were expected to improve themselves out of a job.

Since then, VMMC's leadership has taken a number of steps to reduce tolerance for ambiguity and work-arounds and to make change a regular part of work. To help institutionalize a role for process experts in an organization otherwise filled with experts within disciplines, VMMC created Kaizen Promotion Offices, which support the improvement efforts of its various divisions. To emphasize the idea of quick, constant change, VMMC has conducted several hundred rapid-improvement projects. To make it easy not to work around problems, VMMC created a patient safety alert process, which allows any employee to immediately halt any process that's likely to cause harm to a patient. There's a 24/7 hotline for reporting problems, a "drop and run" commitment from leadership at the department-chief and vice-president levels to immediately respond to the reports and to exhibit a willingness to stop processes until they are fixed. To further bolster the connection between leadership and the "shop floor," department chiefs and managers conduct safety walk-abouts, asking staff to alert them to specific instances in the previous few days of events that prolonged hospitalization, caused a near miss, harmed a patient, or compromised the efforts of people to do their work. Such alerts rose from three per month in 2002, the year the patient safety alert process started, to ten per month in 2003, to 17 per month in 2004. Despite the increase in the number of alerts, the average time to resolution declined from 18 days in 2002 to 13 in 2004.

This commitment to process improvement has indeed increased quality and reduced costs. In 2002, for instance, 34 patients contracted pneumonia in the hospital while on a ventilator, and five of them died. But in 2004, only four such patients became ill, and just one died. Associated costs dropped from $500,000 in

2002 to $60,000 in 2004. And the overall number of professional liability claims plummeted from 363 in 2002 to 47 in 2004. Improved efficiencies in labor, space, and equipment allowed VMMC to avoid adding a new hyperbaric chamber (saving $1 million) and avoid moving its endoscopy suites (saving another $1 million to $3 million), even as it increased the number of patients its oncology unit treated from 120 to 188.

So far, no one can point to a single hospital and say, "There is the Toyota of health care." No organization has fully institutionalized to Toyota's level the ability to design work as experiments, improve work through experiments, share the resulting knowledge through collaborative experimentation, and develop people as experimentalists. But there's reason for optimism. Companies in a host of other industries have already successfully followed in Toyota's footsteps, using common approaches to organizing for continuous learning, improvement, and innovation that transcend their business differences. And these approaches have been successful when piloted in health care.

More to the point, the health care system is populated by bright, dedicated, well-intentioned people. They have already demonstrated a capacity to experiment and learn in order to master the knowledge and skills within their disciplines. One can imagine few people better qualified to master the skills and knowledge needed to improve processes that span the boundaries of their disciplines.

Note

1. John P. Burke, "Infection Control—A Problem for Patient Safety," *New England Journal of Medicine* (February 2003); William R. Jarvis, "Infection Control and Changing Health-Care Delivery Systems," *Emerging Infectious Diseases* (March–April 2001); Robert A. Weinstein, "Nosocomial Infection Update," *Emerging Infectious Diseases* (July–September 1998).

STEVEN J. SPEAR is a senior fellow at the Institute for Healthcare Improvement in Cambridge, Massachusetts.

Originally published in September 2005. Reprint R0509D

Kaiser Permanente's Innovation on the Front Lines

by Lew McCreary

CHRIS MCCARTHY SHOWS UP for an early-morning interview wearing raspberry-colored scrubs. Later he'll head to one of Kaiser Permanente's Bay Area hospitals to watch nurses at work. McCarthy, a KP innovation specialist, is just beginning a project aimed at optimizing the time nurses spend with their patients. He's often in clinical settings, observing how health care providers do their jobs; how they interact with one another, with technology, and with patients; and how patients respond.

McCarthy is part of the Innovation Consultancy, a small team within Kaiser Permanente that was born of the company's involvement with the design firm IDEO. In 2003 KP hired IDEO to help it develop better, more-efficient ways of performing certain high-value

activities, and gained a distinctive innovation methodology in the process.

What McCarthy will do all day is watch people, take
notes, snap pictures, and make sketches. (He's a fly on
the wall, but a very active fly.) Some of what matters to
him will be physical or logistical: Who stands where,
does what, communicates most or least or best? What
tools are used? Are they used easily, effectively, grace-
fully? How are they carried? If they're not carried, are
they conveniently positioned? But McCarthy is also
interested in subjective evidence. He will ask nurses
how they feel about what they're doing and patients
how they feel about what's being done. He will try to get
some sense of the atmosphere—color, light, energy,
mood. He knows that information that may at first seem
unimportant can later mean a lot. So there's an unknown cost to overlooking anything. Or anyone.

After a day spent watching other people work,
McCarthy tries to capture experiences from the points
of view of everyone involved. It's a combination of
anthropology, journalism, and empathy. The goal is to
find hidden clues to the nature of the problem at hand
and some line of inquiry for progressing toward possible solutions.

The Innovation Consultancy takes on carefully chosen projects throughout Kaiser Permanente, which is
based in Oakland, California, and serves the health
needs of more than 8.6 million members in nine states
and the District of Columbia. That's a huge laboratory
for tackling opportunities to improve health care practice. McCarthy and his colleagues pursue an expansive,

Idea in Brief

The Innovation Consultancy, a small team within the health care provider Kaiser Permanente, practices an expansive, service-focused version of innovation that is both rapid and economical in comparison with the conventional version. The team's members observe how health care providers interact with one another, with technology, and with patients, and how the patients respond. They take photographs, draw pictures, write stories, and try to capture experiences from the point of view of everyone involved. During KP MedRite, a project to reduce the error rate in dispensing medication to hospital patients, the team asked nurses what they thought was wrong with the dispensing process. The nurses usually replied, "Nothing." But when given a chance to make self-portraits, they would draw themselves with sad faces and frazzled hair. Interruptions appeared to be the leading cause of errors—so one of the resulting innovations was a bright yellow sash signaling that its wearer was not to be disturbed. KP's Chris McCarthy founded the Innovation Learning Network to accelerate knowledge transfer among peers in the nonprofit health care industry. One promising process that has emerged, Inflection Navigator, helps patients who've received a frightening diagnosis handle the consequent urgent tasks—follow-up tests, visits to specialists, decision making about treatment and care—with the aid of care coordinators. This innovation and others like it arise from a brand of creativity that transcends the media version of the health care debate.

service-focused version of innovation, not the conventional one that by definition excludes everything but new technologies or tangible products. Surprisingly little attention has yet been paid to this version. But, as Kaiser is discovering, the bucks are relatively few and the bang can be disproportionately big. Compared with costly, long-horizon, research-driven innovation, service-focused innovation can be done both rapidly and economically.

If the Innovation Consultancy can be said to have a larger social purpose, it is to improve the quality of health care even beyond Kaiser Permanente's corporate boundaries. Its work is still in a relatively early stage—one in which there may be an abundance of low-hanging fruit. And given the depth and breadth of the problem, widespread improvements may be slow in coming. That's why McCarthy—eager to accelerate the pace of knowledge transfer among peers in the not-for-profit health care space—founded the Innovation Learning Network, a consortium of 16 health care organizations that meet regularly to share ideas and the results of their respective innovation efforts. It remains to be seen whether his goals will be achieved. But the innovators' experimental approach bears watching—no matter what your industry.

Consider, for example, the return on investment from a project called KP MedRite, an effort to reduce medication errors in KP hospitals. Developing it cost about $470,000. The project was designed and piloted in 2007 and had been implemented in 75% of KP's hospitals by early 2008. Since then it has yielded $965,000 in cost avoidance (for care associated with treating the consequences of medication errors). The process has also produced intangible, hard-to-measure benefits such as greater employee satisfaction and patient peace of mind. Savings are bound to grow as MedRite is implemented in the rest of the company's hospitals, with little additional investment required.

Nurse Knowledge Exchange

IDEO made its reputation by practicing "human-centered design" (see "Design Thinking," HBR June 2008). The firm's idea was that you can't successfully innovate in a vacuum; you need to explore the ways people live, what they think, and how they feel about things before you can understand the problem your new product or service should address.

One of the first projects KP did with IDEO was meant to improve how nurses exchanged patient information between shifts—a process that typically took 45 minutes or more and delayed the arriving nurses' first contact with their patients. Not surprisingly, the project revealed that patients felt a "hole in their care" during shift changes. Worse, nurses compiled and exchanged patient information in idiosyncratic and unreliable ways (some even scrawled notes on their scrubs). Important details were often left out, or care that had already been provided was needlessly repeated.

What came to be called Nurse Knowledge Exchange created a process for passing on higher-quality information more quickly and reliably. Now the exchange occurs at the patient's bedside rather than at the nurses' station. Patients are encouraged to participate, making it less likely that anything important relating to their care will fall through the cracks. New software helps nurses compile information in a standard format throughout their shifts. And they are less likely hours later to experience a jolt of panic that they've forgotten to communicate something important. Nurse Knowledge Exchange has since been rolled out to all of KP's hospitals.

As the relationship between KP and IDEO progressed, what had been conceived as a three-month immersion turned into an eighteen-month apprenticeship. "We were trying to mold the DNA of IDEO into Kaiser Permanente, to create a kind of IDEO outpost here," McCarthy says. "By the end of that period it was pretty clear that the methodology worked really well for us."

The Innovation Consultancy was created to help institutionalize what KP had learned from its work with IDEO. At first, says McCarthy, the team supposed it would "sprinkle the method all over the organization," propagating innovation clusters that were familiar with the IDEO way and could initiate projects on their own. He now admits that assumption was naive. First, the methodology isn't so easy to master—after six years of using it, McCarthy says, his group is still learning and perfecting. And, of course, not everyone has the temperament or wants to be an innovator. It's more important for the team to sprinkle something else: an eagerness to try new things. That can be accomplished in part by deputizing line staffers to act as "codesigners" on a project basis.

Uncovering the Untold Story

In too many enterprises, innovation is treated as a sideshow. It may get its due in lip service without being appropriately supported or well understood. Worse, it isn't integrated into the fabric or behavior of the business. Potential breakthrough ideas struggle to survive amid entrenched systems and values. In a 2007 McKinsey Global Survey of more than 1,400 executives, 70% cited innovation as crucial to their companies' future growth, yet only 35% were "very" confident that they could execute innovation successfully. Imagine if 65% of CEOs doubted their company's ability to plan a winning strategy, run its supply chain, or manage its finances.

Kaiser Permanente is among a minority of enterprises that take innovative approaches to innovation itself. Within its industry, Kaiser enjoys some advantages:

It's a self-contained, full-service health care provider with its own hospitals and other facilities, its own network of salaried physicians, and its own insurance plans and administration infrastructure, meaning it can exert relatively frictionless control over all aspects of care for its 8.6 million members.

It has always rejected the now dominant fee-for-service model that is often blamed for rampaging growth in health care costs. Premiums fund whatever care members need. Because KP's physicians are salaried, rather than paid on the basis of how many tests they order or procedures they perform, care is untainted by any economic conflict of interest.

Its enormous member population and the cooperative interlinking of its components enable it to compile massive amounts of evidence for the superiority of certain treatment regimens—and to do so at a level that approaches the ideal of personalized medical care.

It is currently the largest and most advanced private-sector adopter of electronic medical record (EMR) systems. Any member can enter any KP health care facility knowing that all his or her medical data are readily accessible by local clinicians. The database fueled by the EMR system constitutes a rich asset for nearly limitless lines of research.

In this context the Innovation Consultancy flourishes. One key to its success is a form of investigation that McCarthy calls "uncovering the untold story." For example, when asked to say what's wrong with the way medications are dispensed to their hospital patients, nurses will usually answer "nothing." But when they're asked to draw pictures of themselves in the midst of the task, "their frazzled hair is standing up on end," McCarthy says. "So you start exploring with them: 'Why do you draw yourself with a sad face and frazzled hair?' Then they start pouring out what the issues are: 'I'm overworked. I need help during the process. It's chaotic, it's full of interruptions, it's unclear.'"

That's what unfolded during the KP MedRite project. Dispensing meds correctly means giving the right prescribed drug in the right dose to the right patient at the right time. The consequences of medication error can be catastrophic for the patient and very costly for both the institution's reputation and its bottom line.

A 1999 report by the Institute of Medicine ("To Err Is Human: Building a Safer Health System") documented the extent of the problem: Medication errors

How to Package Change

EVERY INNOVATION CONSULTANCY PROJECT includes a "change package"—a set of detailed, clearly written guidebooks that fully describe the innovation, the reasoning behind its creation, the process by which it was developed (with shout-outs to staffers who participated), the benefits it's meant to produce for patients and staff alike, user testimonials gathered during pilot implementations, and the metrics that will be used to evaluate its performance over time. Three different versions of the package target business leaders, project managers, and frontline staff members.

The Institute for Healthcare Improvement—cofounded by the Boston pediatrician and health care reformer Donald Berwick, President Obama's pick to head the Centers for Medicare and Medicaid Services in the Department of Health and Human Services— cited Kaiser Permanente's change packages as best practices in their own right. KP's Chris McCarthy says his company leans on IHI to help it with the back end of innovation. IHI's emphasis is, in part, on making sure that change is well executed and fully embraced. No matter how brilliantly conceived, projects often go awry through neglect of the back-end work.

KP's change packages convey a real-world respect for the challenges and difficulties any innovation can bring. They not only provide sensible instructions for getting on with the program but also reinforce the cultural imperative that change is an important part of work life and innovation ultimately touches every corner of the enterprise.

---

were causing measurable harm to 1.5 million people a year, costing $3.5 billion in additional treatment for resulting injuries, and leading to some 7,000 preventable deaths. The observation phase of the MedRite project strongly suggested that interruptions and distractions were the leading cause of errors. "One nurse trying to give one medication to one person was interrupted 17 times during a single medication pass," McCarthy says.

For nurses, interruptions are a regular feature of hospital life. And they're generally not for idle chitchat about the previous night's Giants game or *Grey's Anatomy* episode. Important information is constantly being asked for and given out. Urgent tasks ebb and flow unpredictably, so distraction can't or shouldn't be eliminated entirely. The challenge for MedRite was to create situational "interruption-free zones" for nurses.

As the project progressed, nurses, physicians, pharmacists, and patients were enlisted in what is known as the deep-dive phase of KP's innovation process. This typically occurs at the Sidney R. Garfield Health Care Innovation Center, Kaiser's brainstorming and prototyping facility in Oakland. For two days a group of 70 deputized codesigners tackled the problem of medication errors. They produced about 400 ideas, ranging from incremental to outlandish. One team proposed a "Med Bed"—a hospital bed equipped with an automated, patient-personalized dispensary unit.

"It was like the Ferrari of beds," says McCarthy. "It had a refrigerator built in. It had a microwave built in. I mean, it was a pretty crazy bed. But they prototyped it at the Garfield Center—stripped down a bed and taped all these devices onto it." The Med Bed wasn't ultimately adopted, but the prototype demonstration clarified desirable features that were incorporated into the eventual solution. "In showing us the process of using the Med Bed," McCarthy says, "what they

Injecting Genius into the Process

THE INDIAN CARDIAC SURGEON Devi Shetty has shown that the speed and efficiency of coronary bypass can be increased without sacrificing the quality of outcomes. His surgeons have done many more operations than others their age who perform conventional bypass surgery, thus enhancing their proficiency.

Furthermore, Shetty's approach—almost in the tradition of time-and-motion studies—parses surgical procedures into their basic elements and actions. The mythic-heroic notion of surgeons as uniquely gifted artists becomes a manufacturing model consisting of choreographed steps performed by a highly skilled team.

The hospitals in India's nonprofit Aravind Eye Care System drive cost out of eye surgery in the same way Shetty drives it out of coronary bypass—by creating surgical assembly lines and innovating processes, techniques, and materials. Revenue from the 30% of their customers who can afford market rates subsidizes free care for the rest.

were really asking for was to have everything within reach."

At the deep dive, he says, "a nurse came up with the idea of a smock that said 'Leave me alone' on it." Numerous prototypes led to one of MedRite's key physical innovations—"no-interruption wear"—a bright-yellow reflective sash that signals that its wearer is not to be disturbed. Another physical innovation involved color on the floor around the central medication dispensary to indicate a "sacred zone" that no one may enter if someone else is already working there. But the main innovation was a five-step process for ensuring that medications are dispensed correctly.

Care Coordinators

KP's emphasis has been on designing better means of delivery, which can improve the quality of care much more dramatically and quickly than any whizbang technology. Such reforms can also save money, by off-loading from expensive clinicians duties that lower-paid staffers can perform. (Kaiser is not without critics who question some of its motives and practices—sometimes alleging that its emphasis on cost control crosses the line into rationed care.)

Lyle Berkowitz is a Chicago primary-care physician who also runs the Szollosi Healthcare Innovation Program, a charitable foundation that belongs to the Innovation Learning Network. Berkowitz has worked with the ILN on a process to help patients who've received a frightening diagnosis more easily negotiate the ensuing flurry of necessary activity: follow-up tests, visits to specialists, decision making about treatment and care.

The process is called Inflection Navigator, because a diagnosis of cancer or serious cardiac disease, for example, presents the patient with a profound inflection point. At such times many patients feel too overwhelmed to ask important questions or undertake important tasks. Inflection Navigator assigns to each patient a care coordinator, who explains, assists, sets up appointments, anticipates questions, and provides answers.

The care coordinator sequences activities to minimize the inconvenience to patients and maximize the value of the time they spend with doctors. For example, a patient's visit to a specialist might be scheduled only after the necessary tests have been done and the results can guide a recommendation. "It decreases the burden on both the patient and the doctor," Berkowitz says.

It also bends the cost curve down. Care coordinators don't have to be highly trained and heavily compensated. They depend on a database of medical protocols reflecting best practices for diagnostic procedures and the latest treatments for various diseases. This frees physicians to spend more time where their expertise makes the greatest difference.

The process bends the learning curve, too. If, say, the standard treatment for atrial fibrillation changes, "the cool thing is I don't have to go and try to educate all my doctors," Berkowitz says. "Because it can take years to do that. All I have to do is change the protocol that's already built into the system." The physician makes the diagnosis and then hands the patient off to the care coordinator.

Democratizing Health Care

Lyle Berkowitz mans one corner of a small booth on the modest show floor of a conference and expo in Boston. The event is a joint production of the Innovation Learning Network and the Center for Integration of Medicine & Innovative Technology, a nonprofit consortium of Boston-area teaching hospitals and engineering schools. The proceedings might best be described as a festival for health care geeks.

Berkowitz is busy explaining Inflection Navigator to interested attendees. The emphasis here is on sharing, not selling. No booth bunnies, blaring music, flashing lights, or branded tchotchkes, just conversation—enough conversation that superior listening skills are needed to hear above the din. The exhibitors have zeal in common. They want to make health care better, smarter, cheaper, and more accessible.

Chris McCarthy hovers and circulates. It's the last day of the event, and he has the semi-relaxed look of someone who has either dodged or dealt with whatever might have gone wrong and is finally surrendering to satisfaction. Sharing real-world evidence of what works—ideas, practices, protocols—exhilarates people like McCarthy and Berkowitz. To them, there's nothing odd about 16 independent organizations coming together to improve more quickly than they could if they were left to themselves. It simply makes sense to spread improvement as broadly as possible.

This is not the vision of health care that emerged in the grinding yet cartoonish debate leading up to the passage of what is now called Obamacare. It was easy then to imagine that the whole system was willfully committed to cruelty, greed, vanity, and ineptitude. Beyond the fray, however, creativity flourishes. McCarthy and others, by democratizing the methods of innovation, are democratizing health care, giving patients and nonphysician caregivers a louder voice in designing the future.

LEW McCREARY is a contributing editor at *Harvard Business Review.*

Originally published in September 2010. Reprint R1009H

Why Innovation in Health Care Is So Hard

by Regina E. Herzlinger

HEALTH CARE—IN THE UNITED STATES, certainly, but also in most other developed countries—is ailing and in need of help. Yes, medical treatment has made astonishing advances over the years. But the packaging and delivery of that treatment are often inefficient, ineffective, and consumer unfriendly.

The well-known problems range from medical errors, which by some accounts are the eighth leading cause of death in the United States, to the soaring cost of health care. The amount spent now represents about one-sixth of the U.S. gross domestic product; it continues to grow much faster than the economy; and it threatens the economic future of the governments, businesses, and individuals called upon to foot the bill. Despite the outlay, more than 40 million people have no health insurance.

Such problems beg for innovative solutions involving every aspect of health care—its delivery to consumers, its technology, and its business models. Indeed, a great deal of money has been spent on the search for solutions. U.S. government spending on health care R&D, which came to $26 billion in 2003, is topped only by the government's spending on defense R&D. Private-sector spending on health care R&D—in pharmaceuticals, biotechnology, medical devices, and health services—also runs into the tens of billions of dollars. According to one study of U.S. companies, only software spawns more new ventures receiving early-stage angel funding than the health field.

Despite this enormous investment in innovation and the magnitude of the opportunity for innovators to both do good and do well, all too many efforts fail, losing billions of investor dollars along the way. Some of the more conspicuous examples: the disastrous outcome of the managed care revolution, the $40 billion lost by investors to biotech ventures, and the collapse of numerous businesses aimed at bringing economies of scale to fragmented physician practices.

So why is innovation so unsuccessful in health care? To answer, we must break down the problem, looking at the different types of innovation and the forces that affect them, for good or ill. (See the sidebar "Six Forces That Can Drive Innovation—Or Kill It.") This method of analysis, while applied here mainly to health care in the U.S., also offers a framework for understanding the health care problems of other developed economies— and for helping managers understand innovation challenges in any industry.

Idea in Brief

If any business could benefit from innovation, it's U.S. health care—with its notoriously expensive, inefficient, and consumer-unfriendly services. Sure, major investments in innovation are under way. The government shelled out $26 billion for health care R&D in 2003 alone. And private-sector spending totals tens of billions of dollars.

Yet despite these enormous investments, many innovation efforts fail—losing billions along the way. The reason? Innovators encounter numerous barriers, including difficulty generating funding, restrictive regulations, and other players seeking to protect their turf. Consider Health Stop, a chain of physician-staffed walk-in clinics that initially generated millions in revenue. Local doctors and nonprofit hospital emergency rooms, resentful of lost business, badmouthed Health Stop's quality of care—eventually driving it out of business.

How to generate the innovations health care desperately needs? Herzlinger recommends identifying the forces that can help or hinder your innovation efforts—then turning them to your advantage. MinuteClinic, for example, escaped Health Stop's fate by providing care through nurse practitioners and treating a limited set of common ailments. Physicians and hospitals didn't view Minute-Clinic as a threat and made no public outcry against it. Result? The company and its innovative business model have thrived. And consumers are benefiting from Minute-Clinic's short waits, low prices, and handy locations.

A Health Care Innovation Catalog

Three kinds of innovation can make health care better and cheaper. One changes the ways *consumers* buy and use health care. Another uses *technology* to develop new products and treatments or otherwise improve care. The third generates new *business models,* particularly those that involve the horizontal or vertical integration of separate health care organizations or activities.

Idea in Practice

To move health care innovations forward, Herzlinger offers these guidelines.

Understand the Forces Affecting Innovation Efforts

- **Players.** Powerful stakeholders can help or attack you—as Health Stop discovered.

- **Funding.** Investors may not be willing to wait the many years required to find out whether an innovative product will get FDA approval. Investors may also be confused by the complexities of the health care industry's third-party payment system.

- **Policy.** Regulators, knowing they'll be punished more for approving a harmful drug than delaying a useful innovation, may block promising new ideas with restrictive policies.

- **Technology.** You'll encounter competition within technology types (such as among different drugs aimed at a disease category) and across technology types. For example, the polio vaccine eliminated the need for drugs, devices, and services formerly used to treat the disease.

- **Customers.** With ready access to comparative information about drugs, diagnostics, services, and devices, consumers may embrace or reject innovations independent of your marketing efforts.

- **Accountability.** You risk a backlash if you don't address the demands of agencies that audit the health care industry's performance—such as the National Committee for Quality Assurance and the Joint Commission on Accreditation of Healthcare Organizations.

Consumer-Focused

Innovations in the delivery of health care can result in more-convenient, more-effective, and less-expensive treatments for today's time-stressed and increasingly empowered health care consumers. For example, a health plan can involve consumers in the service delivery process by offering low-cost, high-deductible

Manage Those Forces—and Overcome Them

Any health care innovation—whether focused on satisfying consumers, developing a new technology, or designing a better business model—stands a better chance of succeeding when you manage the forces that affect innovation efforts.

Example: When medical technology company Medtronic expanded into implantable heart defibrillators, it worked directly with the surgeons who would be implanting them, identifying technical problems and setting procedures. It confirmed the device's safety and efficacy with clinical trials, simplifying reimbursement approval from insurers. And it developed a technology for which there were no competing offerings. Its savvy navigation of innovation barriers enabled it to branch into numerous other medical and surgical devices.

Example: Health care facilities chain HCA successfully pioneered an innovative business model by consolidating management of hospitals and outpatient centers. HCA wisely avoided competing directly with politically powerful academic medical centers. Instead, it expanded into underserved communities, where customers appreciated a local hospital and doctors welcomed the chance to work in modern facilities. Even after weathering a fraud investigation in the late 1990s, the publicly traded company, with a new management team, has continued to perform well in the stock market.

insurance, which can give members greater control over their personal health care spending. Or a health plan (or service provider) can focus on becoming more user-friendly. Patients, after all, are like other consumers: They want not only a good product—quality care at a good price—but also ease of use. People in the United States have to wait an average of three weeks for

Six Forces That Can Drive Innovation— or Kill It

Players

The friends and foes lurking in the health care system that can destroy or bolster an innovation's chance of success.

Funding

The processes for generating revenue and acquiring capital, both of which differ from those in most other industries.

Policy

The regulations that pervade the industry, because incompetent or fraudulent suppliers can do irreversible human damage.

Technology

The foundation for advances in treatment and for innovations that can make health care delivery more efficient and convenient.

Customers

The increasingly engaged consumers of health care, for whom the passive term "patient" seems outdated.

Accountability

The demand from vigilant consumers and cost-pressured payers that innovative health care products be not only safe and effective but also cost-effective relative to competing products.

---

an appointment and, when they show up, 30 minutes to see a doctor, according to a 2003 study by the American Medical Association. More seriously, they often must travel from one facility to another for treatment, especially in the case of chronic diseases that involve several medical disciplines.

Technology

New drugs, diagnostic methods, drug delivery systems, and medical devices offer the hope of better treatment and of care that is less costly, disruptive, and painful. For example, implanted sensors can help patients monitor their diseases more effectively. And IT innovations that connect the many islands of information in the health care system can both vastly improve quality and lower costs by, for example, keeping a patient's various providers informed and thereby reducing errors of omission or commission.

Business Model

Health care is still an astonishingly fragmented industry. More than half of U.S. physicians work in practices of three or fewer doctors; a quarter of the nation's 5,000 community hospitals and nearly half of its 17,000 nursing homes are independent; and the medical device and biotechnology sectors are made up of thousands of small firms. Innovative business models, particularly those that integrate health care activities, can increase efficiency, improve care, and save consumers time. You can roll a number of independent players up into a single organization—horizontal integration—to generate economies of scale. Or you can bring the treatment of a chronic disease under one roof—vertical integration—and make the treatment more effective and convenient. In the latter case, patients get one-stop shopping and are freed from the burden of coordinating their care with myriad providers (for example, the ophthalmologists, podiatrists, cardiologists, neurologists, and nephrologists who care for diabetics). Such "focused factories," to adopt C. Wickham Skinner's term, cut costs by improving patients' health. Furthermore, they reduce the likelihood that an individual's care will fall between the cracks of different medical disciplines.

The health care system erects an array of barriers to each of these valuable types of innovation. More often than not, though, the obstacles can be overcome by managing the six forces that have an impact on health care innovation.

The Forces Affecting Innovation

The six forces—industry players, funding, public policy, technology, customers, and accountability—can help or hinder efforts at innovation. Individually or in combination, the forces will affect the three types of innovation in different ways.

Players

The health care sector has many stakeholders, each with an agenda. Often, these players have substantial resources and the power to influence public policy and opinion by attacking or helping the innovator. For example, hospitals and doctors sometimes blame technology-driven product innovators for the health care system's high costs. Medical specialists wage turf warfare for control of patient services, and insurers battle medical service and technology providers over which treatments and payments are acceptable. Inpatient hospitals and outpatient care providers vie for patients, while chains and independent organizations spar over market influence. Nonprofit, for-profit, and publicly funded institutions quarrel over their respective roles and rights. Patient advocates seek influence with policy makers and politicians, who may have a different agenda altogether—namely, seeking fame and public adulation through their decisions or votes.

The competing interests of the different groups aren't always clear or permanent. The AMA and the tort lawyers, bitter foes on the subject of physician malpractice, have lobbied together for legislation to enable people who are wrongly denied medical care to sue managed-care insurance plans. Unless innovators recognize and try to work with the complex interests of the different players, they will see their efforts stymied.

Funding
Innovation in health care presents two kinds of financial challenges: funding the innovation's development and figuring out who will pay how much for the product or service it yields. One problem is the long investment time needed for new drugs or therapies that require FDA approval. While venture capitalists backing an IT start-up may be able to get their money out in two to three years, investors in a biotech firm have to wait ten years even to find out whether a product will be approved for use. Another problem is that many traditional sources of capital aren't familiar with the health care industry, so it's difficult to find investors, let alone investors who can provide helpful guidance to the innovator.

A frequent source of investor confusion is the health care sector's complex system of payments, or reimbursements, which typically come not from the ultimate consumer but from a third party—the government or a private insurer. This arrangement raises an array of issues. Most obviously, insurers must approve a new product or service, and its pricing, before they will pay. And their perception of a product's value, which determines the level of reimbursement, may differ from patients'. Furthermore, insurers may disagree. Medicare, whose relationships with its enrollees sometimes last decades, may see far more value in an innovation with a long-term cost impact, such as an obesity reduction treatment or an expensive diagnostic test, than would a commercial insurer, which typically sees an annual 20% turnover. An additional complication: Innovations need to appeal to doctors, who are in a position to recommend new products to patients, and doctors' opinions differ. From a financial perspective, a physician who is paid a flat salary by a health maintenance organization may be less interested in, say, performing a procedure to implant a monitoring device than would a doctor who is paid a fee for such services.

Policy

Government regulation of health care can sometimes aid innovation ("orphan drug" laws provide incentives to companies that develop treatments for rare diseases) and sometimes hinder it (recent legislation in the United States placed a moratorium on the opening of new specialty hospitals that focus on certain surgical procedures). Thus, it is important for innovators to understand the extensive network of regulations that may affect a particular innovation and how and by whom those rules are enacted, modified, and applied. For instance, officials know they will be punished by the public and politicians more for underregulating—approving a harmful drug, say—than for tightening the approval process, even if doing so delays a useful innovation.

A company with a new health care idea should also be aware that regulators, to demonstrate their value to the public, may ripple their muscles occasionally by tightly interpreting ambiguous rules or punishing a hapless innovator.

Technology

As medical technology evolves, understanding how and when to adopt or invest in it is critically important. Move too early, and the infrastructure needed to support the innovation may not yet be in place; wait too long, and the time to gain competitive advantage may have passed.

Keep in mind that competition exists not only within each technology—among drugs aimed at a disease category, for example—but also across different technologies. The polio vaccine eventually eliminated the need for drugs, devices, and services that had been used to treat the disease, just as kidney transplants have reduced the need for dialysis. Conversely, the discovery of an effective molecular diagnostic method for a disease such as Alzheimer's would greatly enhance the demand for therapeutic drugs and devices.

Customers

The empowered and engaged consumers of health care—
the passive "patient" increasingly seems an anachronis-
tic term—are a force to be reckoned with in all three types
of health care innovation. Sick people and their families
join disease associations such as the American Cancer
Society that lobby for research funds. Interest groups,
such as the elderly, advocate increased funding for
their health care needs through powerful organizations
such as AARP. Those who suffer from various ailments
pressure health care providers for access to drugs, diagnostics, services, and devices they consider effective.

What's more, consumers spend tremendous sums
out of their own pockets on health care services—for
example, an estimated $40 billion on complementary
medicine such as acupuncture and meditation—that
many traditional medical providers believe to be of
dubious value. Armed with information gleaned from
the Internet, such consumers disregard medical advice
they don't agree with, choosing, for example, to shun
certain drugs doctors have prescribed. A company that
recognizes and leverages consumers' growing sense of
empowerment, and actual power, can greatly enhance
the adoption of an innovation.

Accountability

Increasingly, empowered consumers and cost-pressured payers are demanding accountability from health
care innovators. For instance, they require that technology innovators show cost-effectiveness and long-term
safety, in addition to fulfilling the shorter-term efficacy

and safety requirements of regulatory agencies. In the United States, the numerous industry organizations that have been created to meet these demands haven't fully succeeded in doing so. For example, a study found that the accreditation of hospitals by the Joint Commission on Accreditation of Healthcare Organizations (JCAHO), an industry-dominated group, had scant correlation with mortality rates.

One reason for the limited success of these agencies is that they typically focus on process rather than on output, looking, say, not at improvements in patient health but at whether a provider has followed a treatment process. However well intentioned, these bodies usually aren't neutral auditors focused on the consumer but rather are extensions of the industries they regulate. For instance, JCAHO and the National Committee for Quality Assurance, the agencies primarily responsible for monitoring compliance with standards in the hospital and insurance sectors, are overseen mainly by the firms in those industries.

But whether the agents of accountability are effective or not, health care innovators must do everything possible to try to address their often opaque demands. Otherwise, innovating companies face the prospect of a forceful backlash from industry monitors or the public.

The Barriers to Innovation

Unless the six forces are acknowledged and managed intelligently, any of them can create obstacles to innovation in each of the three areas.

In Consumer-Focused Innovation

The existence of hostile industry *players* or the absence of helpful ones can hinder consumer-focused innovation. Status quo organizations tend to view such innovation as a direct threat to their power. For example, many physicians resent direct-to-consumer pharmaceutical advertising or for-profit attempts to provide health care in convenient locations, such as shopping malls, and use their influence to resist such moves. Conversely, companies' attempts to reach consumers with new products or services are often thwarted by a lack of developed consumer marketing and distribution channels in the health care sector as well as a lack of intermediaries, such as distributors, who would make the channels work. Opponents of consumer-focused innovation may try to influence public *policy,* often by playing on the general bias against for-profit ventures in health care or by arguing that a new type of service, such as a facility specializing in one disease, will cherry-pick the most profitable customers and leave the rest to nonprofit hospitals. Innovators must therefore be prepared to respond to those seeking *accountability* for a new product's or new service's cost-effectiveness, efficacy, and safety.

It also can be difficult for innovators to get *funding* for consumer-focused ventures because few traditional health care investors have significant expertise in products and services marketed to and purchased by the consumer. This hints at another financial challenge: Consumers generally aren't used to paying for conventional health care. While they may not blink at the purchase of a $35,000 SUV—or even a medical service not traditionally covered by insurance, such as cosmetic surgery or vitamin supplements—many will hesitate to fork over $1,000 for a medical image. Insurers and other third-party payers also may resist footing the bill for some consumer-focused services—for example, increased diagnostic testing—fearing a further increase in their costs.

These barriers impeded—and ultimately helped kill or drive into the arms of a competitor—two companies that offered innovative health care services directly to consumers. Health Stop was a venture capital–financed chain of conveniently located, no-appointment-needed health care centers in the eastern and midwestern U.S. for patients who were seeking fast medical treatment and did not require hospitalization. Although designed to serve people who had no primary care doctor or who needed treatment on nights and weekends, Health Stop unwittingly found itself competing with local community doctors and nonprofit hospital emergency rooms for business.

Guess who won? The community doctors bad-mouthed Health Stop's quality of care and its faceless corporate ownership, while the hospitals argued in the media that their emergency rooms could not survive without revenue from the relatively healthy patients whom Health Stop targeted. The criticism tarnished the chain in the eyes of some patients. Because Health Stop hadn't fully anticipated this opposition, it hadn't worked in advance with the local physicians and hospitals to resolve problems and to sufficiently document to the medical community the quality of its care. The company's failure to foresee these setbacks was compounded by the lack of health services expertise of its major investor, a venture capital firm that typically bankrolled high-tech start-ups. Although the chain had more than 100 clinics and generated annual sales of more than $50 million during its heyday, it was never profitable. The business was dissolved after a decade.

HealthAllies, founded as a health care "buying club" in 1999, met a similar fate. By aggregating purchases of medical services not typically covered by insurance—such as orthodontia, in vitro fertilization, and plastic surgery—it hoped to negotiate discounted rates with providers, thereby giving individual customers, who paid a small referral fee, the collective clout of an insurance company. It was a classic do-good, do-well venture, but it failed to flourish.

The main obstacle was the health care industry's absence of marketing and distribution channels for individual consumers. Potential intermediaries weren't sufficiently interested. For many employers, adding this service to the subsidized insurance they already offered employees would have meant new administrative hassles with little benefit. Insurance brokers found the commissions for selling the service—a small percentage of a small referral fee—unattractive, especially as customers were purchasing the right to participate for a one-time medical need rather than renewable policies. Without marketing channels, the company found that its customer acquisition costs were too high. HealthAllies was bought for a modest amount in 2003.

UnitedHealth Group, the giant insurance company that took it over, has found ready buyers for the company's service among the many employers it already sells insurance to.

In Technology-Based Innovation

The obstacles to technological innovations are numerous. On the *accountability* front, an innovator faces the complex task of complying with a welter of often murky governmental regulations, which increasingly require companies to show that new products not only do what's claimed, safely, but also are cost-effective relative to competing products.

As for *funding,* the innovator must work with insurers in advance of a launch to see to it that the product will be eligible for reimbursement (usually easier if it's used in treatment than if it's for diagnostic purposes). In seeking this approval, the innovator will typically look for support from industry *players*—physicians, hospitals, and an array of powerful intermediaries, including group purchasing organizations, or GPOs, which consolidate the purchasing power of thousands of hospitals. GPOs typically favor suppliers with broad product lines rather than a single innovative product. The intermediaries also include pharmaceutical benefit managers, or PBMs, which create "formularies" for health insurers—that is, the menu of drugs that will be made available at relatively low prices to enrollees.

Innovators must also take into account the economics of insurers and health care providers and the relationships among them. For instance, insurers do not typically pay separately for capital equipment; payments for procedures that use new equipment must cover the capital costs in addition to the hospital's other expenses. So a vendor of a new anesthesia technology must be ready to help its hospital customers obtain additional reimbursement from insurers for the higher costs of the new devices.

Even technologies that unambiguously reduce costs—by substituting capital for labor, say, or shortening the length of a hospital stay—face challenges. Because insurers tend to analyze their costs in silos, they often don't see the link between a reduction in hospital labor costs and the new technology responsible for it; they see only the new costs associated with the technology. For example, insurers may resist approving an expensive new heart drug even if, over the long term, it will decrease their payments for cardiac-related hospital admissions.

Innovators must also take pains to identify the best parties to target for adoption of a new technology and then provide them with complete medical and financial information. Traditionally trained surgeons, for instance, may take a dim view of what are known as minimally invasive surgery, or MIS, techniques, which enable radiologists and other nonsurgeons to perform operations. In the early days of MIS, a spate of articles that could be interpreted as an attempt by surgeons to protect their turf appeared in the *New England Journal of Medicine* claiming the techniques would cause an explosion of unneeded surgeries.

A little-appreciated barrier to technology innovation involves *technology* itself—or, rather, innovators' tendency to be infatuated with their own gadgets and blind to competing ideas. While an innovative product may indeed offer an effective treatment that would save money, particular providers and insurers might, for a variety of reasons, prefer a completely different technology.

One technology-driven medical device firm saw a major product innovation foiled by several such obstacles. The company's product, an instrument for performing noninvasive surgery to correct acid reflux disease, simplified an expensive and complicated operation, enabling gastroenterologists to perform a procedure usually reserved for surgeons. The device would have allowed surgeons to increase the number of acid reflux procedures they performed. But instead of going to the surgeons to get their buy-in, the company targeted only gastroenterologists for training, setting off a turf war. The firm also failed to work out with insurers a means to obtain coverage and payment—it didn't even obtain a new billing code for the device—before marketing the product. Without these reimbursement protocols in place, physicians and hospitals were reluctant to quickly adopt the new procedure.

Perhaps the biggest barrier was the company's failure to consider a formidable but less-than-obvious competing technology, one that involved no surgery at all. It was an approach that might be called the "Tums solution." Antacids like Tums—and, even more effectively, drugs like Pepcid and Zantac, which had recently come off patent—provided some relief and were deemed good enough by many consumers. As a result, the technologically innovative device for noninvasive surgery was adopted very slowly, permitting rival firms to enter the field.

Similarly, a company that developed a cochlear implant for the profoundly deaf was so infatuated with the technology that it didn't foresee opposition from militant segments of the hearing-impaired community that objected to the concept of a technological "fix" for deafness.

In Business Model Innovation

The integration of health care activities—consolidating the practices of independent physicians, say, or integrating the disparate treatments of a particular disease—can lower costs and improve care. But doing this isn't easy. Many management firms that sought to horizontally integrate physician practices are now bankrupt. And specialty facilities designed to vertically integrate the treatment of a particular disease, from prevention to cure, have generally lost money.

As with consumer-focused innovations, ventures that experiment with new business models often face opposition from local hospitals, physicians, and other industry *players* for whom such innovation poses a competitive threat. Powerful community-based providers that might be harmed by a larger or more efficient rival work to undermine the venture, often playing the public *policy* card by raising antitrust concerns or making the most of prejudices or laws against physician-owned businesses.

Nonprofit health services providers cannot easily merge, because they tend to lack the capital to buy one another. While capital is usually available for *funding* for-profit ventures that are based on horizontal consolidation, vertically integrated organizations may encounter greater difficulties in securing investment, because there typically isn't reimbursement for integrated treatment of a disease (think of breast cancer). Instead, payment is piecemeal. Although Duke University Medical Center's specialized congestive heart failure program reduced the average cost of treating patients by $8,600, or about 40%, by improving their outcomes and therefore their hospital admission rates, the facility was penalized by insurers, which pay for care of the sick and not for improving people's health status. The healthier its patients were, the more money Duke lost.

Technology also plays a part in the success or failure of such operations. Without a robust IT infrastructure, an organization won't be able to deliver the promised benefits of integration. This may not be immediately obvious to people in the health care industry, which is near the bottom of the ladder in terms of IT spending and uniform data standards.

Such obstacles contributed to the problems of MedCath, a North Carolina–based for-profit chain of hospitals specializing in cardiac surgical procedures. In each of the 12 markets where it opened in the late 1990s and early 2000s, the company faced resistance from general-purpose hospitals. They argued that instead of offering cheaper care and better outcomes because of its specialized focus (as the company claimed), MedCath was simply skimming the profitable patients. In some

Prescriptions for Public Policy

IN THE UNITED STATES, a few policy changes would jump-start the health care industry's ability to innovate.

Universal Coverage

Ensuring that the 46 million or so uninsured people in the U.S. have health insurance would spur innovation by dramatically increasing the size of the market. But is it achievable? Universal coverage is, after all, one of the most contentious political issues of our time. Switzerland offers some possible answers. The country requires people to buy health insurance, subsidizing the sick and those who can't afford coverage. Although the Swiss government constrains the design of benefits, Swiss insurers have greater incentives to respond to consumer needs than do U.S. insurers, which sell primarily to employers or to government-based organizations. Switzerland's excellent health care system costs only 11% of GDP, versus 16% for the United States. More detail on the Swiss experience can be found in an article I coauthored, "Consumer-Driven Health Care: Lessons from Switzerland" (*Journal of the American Medical Association,* September 8, 2004).

A Consumer-Driven System

Giving U.S. consumers control over their health insurance spending would transform the health insurance market, better aligning consumers' and innovators' interests. We are already seeing this in the case of the increasingly popular low-cost, high-deductible health insurance policies offered by many employers. To create a completely consumer-driven system, we'd need to replace tax laws favoring employer-based insurance with individual tax

cases, local hospitals strong-armed commercial insurers into excluding MedCath from their lists of approved providers, threatening to cut their own ties with the insurers if they failed to blackball MedCath.

credits for health insurance spending, thereby prompting the transfer of funds that employers currently spend on employee health insurance to the employees themselves.

Market-Based Pricing

A system in which insurers set the prices that providers charge consumers is inefficient and a barrier to innovative attempts to integrate health care activities. Think of Duke University Medical Center's innovative congestive heart failure program: The problem has been that the more patients it could successfully treat without lengthy and expensive hospital admissions, the less money it would make in insurance reimbursement. Disincentives to provide lower-cost care are common; making patients healthy usually doesn't pay. And integrating care—offering the medical equivalent of an automobile, rather than a wheel, an engine, and a chassis—typically doesn't have a reimbursement code.

An SEC for Health Care

In a consumer-driven health care market, how can you shop if you don't know the prices or, more important, the quality of what you're buying? The best mechanism for transparency exists in the financial markets in the form of the U.S. Securities and Exchange Commission. While it has its flaws, the SEC generally ensures that consumers have adequate information by requiring companies to publish financial results that are verified by an independent auditor. In health care, the outcome data of individual providers of care are rarely available, and, when they are, they may be of dubious integrity because they aren't audited by certified, independent professionals.

The resistance was further fueled by resentment among local doctors toward MedCath physicians, all of whom were part owners of the chain. The ownership issue also raised problems on another front. Spurred by arguments that conflicts of interest were unavoidable at MedCath and other physician-owned hospitals, Congress in 2003 placed a moratorium on the future growth of such facilities.

Avoiding the Obstacles

Only legislators can remove the barriers to health care innovation that are the result of current laws and regulations (see the sidebar "Prescriptions for Public Policy"). But companies are far from helpless. A few simple steps can position your business to thrive, despite the obstacles. First, recognize the six forces. Next, turn them to your advantage, if possible. If not, work around them, or, if necessary, concede that a particular innovative venture may not be worth pursuing, at least for now.

MinuteClinic, a Minneapolis-based chain of walk-in clinics located in retail settings such as Target stores, avoided some of the obstacles that hobbled Health Stop in its effort at *consumer-focused innovation*. Like Health Stop, MinuteClinic offers basic health care designed with the needs of cost-conscious and time-pressed consumers in mind. It features short waits and low prices—even lower than Health Stop's, because MinuteClinic treats only a limited set of common ailments (such as strep throat and bladder infections) that don't require expensive equipment. But the big difference is that MinuteClinic hasn't antagonized local physicians. Because care is provided by nurse practitioners, the company doesn't represent a direct competitive threat. Although some doctors have grumbled that nurse practitioners might fail to spot more serious problems, especially in infants, there has been no widespread outcry against MinuteClinic, making the establishment of in-network relationships with major health plans relatively easy.

Medtronic was one of the first makers of implantable heart pacemakers, but over the years, the Minneapolis-based company branched into other medical and surgical devices. The company's success is partly based on its ability to avoid some of the barriers to *technology innovation* that beset the previously mentioned developer of an acid-reflux device. For example, when Medtronic expanded into implantable heart defibrillators, it worked directly with the surgeons who would be implanting them so that the company could identify problems and set procedures. It confirmed the devices' safety and efficacy in clinical trials, which greatly simplified reimbursement approval from insurers. And, of course, there was no effective Tums equivalent as an alternative.

HCA (originally known as Hospital Corporation of America) successfully pioneered a *business model innovation* that allowed it to consolidate the management of dozens of facilities and thereby realize economies of scale unknown in the fragmented health care industry. The national chain—currently 190 hospitals and 200 outpatient centers—succeeded in part because it didn't try to compete head-to-head with politically powerful academic medical centers. Instead, it grew mostly through expansion into underserved communities, where customers were grateful for a local hospital and where doctors welcomed the chance to work in modern facilities. The certainty of reimbursement from insurers and Medicare enabled HCA to borrow heavily for construction, and its access to the equity markets as a public company offered funding that was unavailable to nonprofit hospitals. In the late 1990s, HCA was investigated for Medicare and Medicaid fraud and paid a settlement of $1.7 billion, the largest fraud settlement in U.S. history. No criminal charges were brought against the company, and some people wondered whether a nonprofit institution would have paid so dearly for its alleged misdeeds. But the publicly traded company weathered the crisis and, with a new management team in place, has continued to perform well.

An All-Purpose Treatment

The framework described in this article—the three types of health care innovation and the six forces that affect them—offers a useful way to examine the barriers to innovation in health care systems outside the United States, too. For example, in certain European countries, the government's role as the primary payer for health care has created a different interplay among the six forces.

For obvious reasons, the single-payer system hinders customer-focused innovation. But it also seriously constrains technology-based innovation. The government's need to strictly control costs translates into less money to spend on care of the truly sick, who are the target of most technology-based innovation. Consequently, a large venture-capital community hasn't grown up in

Europe to fund new health technology ventures. Centralized health care systems, with their buying clout, also keep drug and medical device prices low—delighting consumers but squeezing margins for innovators. The centralized nature of the systems would seem to offer the potential for innovation in the treatment of diseases where a lot of integration is needed, but the record is mixed.

Modified to fit the situation, this framework can also be used to analyze the barriers to innovation in a variety of industries. Cataloging the types of innovation that can add value in particular fields and identifying the forces that aid and undermine those advances can uncover insights on how to treat chronic innovation ills—prescriptions that will make any industry healthier.

REGINA E. HERZLINGER is the Nancy R. McPherson Professor of Business Administration at Harvard Business School.

Originally published in May 2006. Reprint R0605B

Will Disruptive Innovations Cure Health Care?

by Clayton M. Christensen, Richard M.J. Bohmer, and John Kenagy

IMAGINE A PORTABLE, low-intensity X-ray machine that can be wheeled between offices on a small cart. It creates images of such clarity that pediatricians, internists, and nurses can detect cracks in bones or lumps in tissue in their offices, not in a hospital. It works through a patented "nanocrystal" process, which uses night-vision technology borrowed from the military. At 10% of the cost of a conventional X-ray machine, it could save patients, their employers, and insurance companies hundreds of thousands of dollars every year. Great innovation, right? Guess again. When the entrepreneur who developed the machine tried to license the technology to established health care companies, he couldn't even get his foot in the door. Large-scale X-ray equipment suppliers wanted no part of it. Why? Because it threatened their business models.

What happened to the X-ray entrepreneur is all too common in the health care industry. Powerful institutional forces fight simpler alternatives to expensive care because those alternatives threaten their livelihoods. And those opponents to low-cost change are usually lined up three or four deep. Imagine for a moment that our entrepreneur was able to license the technology. Even then, he would probably face insuperable barriers. Regulators, afraid of putting patients at risk, would withhold approvals. Radiologists, who establish the licensing standards that regulators enforce, don't want to lose their jobs, so they'd fight it, too. Insurance companies, which approve only established licensed procedures, would refuse to reimburse for it. And hospitals, with their large investments in radiology and emergency departments, want injuries to flow to them—so they, too, would join the forces holding back change.

This resistance to low-cost alternatives is understandable, but it's not in the best interests of the industry or of the patients it serves. Quite the reverse—the health care industry desperately needs to open its doors to market forces. Health care professionals often shudder when they hear that phrase "market forces." But when we use it, we're not talking about letting insurance companies micromanage doctors as they practice medicine or about putting profits above patient care. Rather, we're talking about being open to disruptive technologies and business models that may threaten the status quo but will ultimately raise the quality of health care for everyone.

Idea in Brief

The U.S. health care industry is ailing. The symptoms? Expensive, inconvenient delivery systems that leave more and more consumers dissatisfied. Why? Major health care institutions have "overshot" the level of care most patients need. Researchers and practitioners focus on the most complicated diseases, while paying insufficient attention to the needs of patients with more common ailments.

The cure? All health care industry players must embrace **disruptive innovations**: cheaper, simpler, more convenient products or services that ultimately let less expensive professionals provide sophisticated service in affordable settings. Consider angioplasty, used by cardiologists with patients who not long ago would have needed invasive, costly surgery by open-heart specialists. Or the latest blood glucose meters, which allow diabetic patients to monitor their own health—accurately, conveniently, and inexpensively.

We need many more of these disruptive innovations to revitalize the health care industry. Companies that develop them will grow profitably with less investment. Hospitals and managed-care institutions will stem their financial hemorrhaging. When industry players and consumers join forces to promote affordable, high-quality medical services, everyone will win.

Make no mistake: the U.S. health care industry is in crisis. Prestigious teaching hospitals lose millions of dollars every year. Health care delivery is convoluted, expensive, and often deeply dissatisfying to consumers. Managed care, which evolved to address some of these problems, seems increasingly to contribute to them—and some of the best managed-care agencies are on the brink of insolvency. We believe that a whole host of disruptive innovations, small and large, could end the crisis—but only if the entrenched powers get out of the way and let market forces play out. If the natural

Idea in Practice

Disruptive innovations in other industries offer lessons for transforming health care.

Create a system that matches clinicians' skill levels to the level of medical difficulty.

Use technology to channel simple problems (e.g., strep throat) to clinicians who can follow predictable rules for diagnosis and treatment. For example, expand nurse practitioners' role as primary care providers and provide tools that allow them to accurately refer more complicated conditions to physicians with more sophisticated diagnostic abilities.

Invest more money in technologies that simplify complex problems, and less in high-end technologies.

Today most R&D dollars go to complex solutions for complex problems. But more venture capital must flow to projects focused on technologies that simplify diagnosis and treatment—especially of common diseases. By launching a series of such disruptive business ventures, major health care companies (Johnson & Johnson, Baxter, Merck) could spur significant growth—with less investment.

Don't be afraid to invent the institution that could put you out of business.

We'll always need some general hospitals for critical care (just as we still need mainframe computers after PCs transformed that industry). But most health care needs can be better met through specialized institutions that provide state-of-the-art care for a single category of disorders, such as cardiac or renal illnesses.

Overcome the inertia of regulation.

Instead of working to preserve the existing system at all costs, regulators should be asking, "How can we enable disruptive innovations to emerge?"

Example: An entrepreneur creates a portable X-ray machine for use in medical offices rather than in hospitals—promising cost savings. Regulators could support the new technology and address any concerns about possible risks. How? Require that all images interpreted by nonradiologists be transmitted via Internet to a second-opinion center. There, skilled radiologists could check or confirm initial diagnoses.

process of disruption is allowed to proceed, we'll be able to build a new system that's characterized by lower costs, higher quality, and greater convenience than could ever be achieved under the old system.

What's Wrong with Health Care

In any industry, a disruptive innovation sneaks in from below. While the dominant players are focused on improving their products or services to the point where the average consumer doesn't even know what she's using (think overengineered computers), they miss simpler, more convenient, and less costly offerings initially designed to appeal to the low end of the market. Over time, the simpler offerings get better—so much better that they meet the needs of the vast majority of users. We've seen this happen recently in the telecommunications industry, where routers—initially dismissed by leading makers of the faster, more reliable circuit switches—came to take over the market.

The exhibit "The progress of disruptive innovation" illustrates this dynamic. The top solid line depicts the pace of technological innovation—the improvement an industry creates as it introduces new and more-advanced products to serve the more-sophisticated customers at the high end of the market. We call these *sustaining innovations*. The shaded area outlines the rate of improvement consumers can absorb over the same time. The pace of sustaining innovation nearly always outstrips the ability of customers to absorb it. That creates the potential for upstart companies to introduce

The progress of disruptive innovation

Dominant players in most markets focus on sustaining innovations— on improving their products and services to meet the needs of the profitable high-end customers. Soon, those improvements overshoot the needs of the vast majority of customers. That makes a market ripe for upstart companies seeking to introduce disruptive innovations— cheaper, simpler, more convenient products or services aimed at the lower end of the market. Over time, those products improve to meet the needs of most of the market, a phenomenon that has caused many of history's best companies to plunge into crisis.

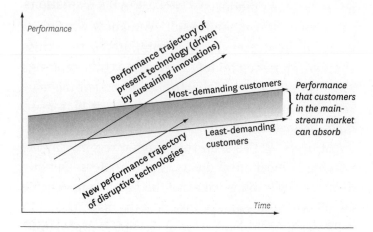

disruptive innovations—cheaper, simpler, more convenient products or services that start by meeting the needs of less-demanding customers. The progress of these disruptive innovations is shown by the bottom solid line. Disruptive technologies have caused many of history's best companies to plunge into crisis and ultimately fail.[1]

This phenomenon of overshooting the needs of average customers and creating the potential for disruption quite accurately describes the health care industry. If we were to draw a graph to illustrate health care specifically, we would measure the complexity of diagnosing and treating various disorders on the vertical axis. The least-demanding tiers of the market are patients with disorders such as simple infectious diseases. The most-demanding tiers include patients with complex, interactive problems such as an elderly man with a broken hip complicated by poor health from long-standing diabetes, hypertension, and heart disease—situations in which multiple systems of the body are involved, and cause and effect are difficult to disentangle.

Our major health care institutions—medical schools, groups of specialist physicians, general hospitals, research organizations—have together overshot the level of care actually needed or used by the vast majority of patients. Indeed, most players in today's health care system are in a lockstep march toward the most scientifically demanding challenges. Between 1960 and now, for example, our medical schools and residency programs have churned out specialists and subspecialists with extraordinary capabilities. But most of the things that afflict us are relatively straightforward disorders whose diagnoses and treatments tap but a small fraction of what our medical schools have prepared physicians to do. Similarly, the vast majority of research funding from the National Institutes of Health is aimed at learning to cure diseases that historically have been incurable. Much less is being spent on learning how to provide the health care that most of us need most of the time in a way that is simpler, more convenient, and less costly.

General hospitals—especially teaching hospitals—have likewise overshot the needs of most patients. Their impressive technological ability to deliver care enables them to address the needs of a relatively small population of very sick patients. But in the process of adding and incurring the costs of such capabilities, they have come to overserve the needs of the much larger population of patients with less serious disorders. Most types of patients that occupied hospital beds 20 years ago are not there today; they're being treated in lower cost, more-focused settings. As the stand-alone cardiac care centers, outpatient surgery centers, and other focused institutions get better and better, they become the price setters. As a consequence, the old high-cost institutions can't compete financially; nor are there enough really sick people to sustain them. Last year not a single teaching hospital in Massachusetts made money.

As a group, the medical schools, specialist physicians, hospitals, and equipment suppliers have done an exceptional job of learning to treat and resolve difficult, intractable problems at the high end. We stand in awe of what they have accomplished. But precisely because of their achievements, health care is now ripe for disruption.

How Disruptive Innovations Work

To get a sense of what those disruptions might be, let's look briefly at what has happened in other industries. Many of the most powerful innovations that disrupted other industries did so by enabling a larger population of less-skilled people to do in a more convenient, less expensive setting things that historically could be performed only by expensive specialists in centralized, inconvenient locations.

For example, in the 1960s when people needed computing help, they had to take their punched cards to the corporate mainframe computer center and wait in line for the data-processing specialists to run the job for them. Minicomputers and then personal computers were disruptive technologies to the mainframe makers. At the outset, they weren't nearly as capable as mainframes, and as a consequence the professionals who operated the sophisticated computers, and the companies that supplied them, discounted their value. But minicomputers enabled engineers to solve problems for themselves that had required centralized computing facilities. And personal computers enabled the unwashed masses—less-skilled people like the rest of us—to compute in the convenience of their offices and homes.

Nearly every disruptive innovation in history has had the same impact. George Eastman's camera made amateur photography widespread. Bell's telephone let people communicate without the need for professional telegraph operators. Photocopying enabled office workers to do things that historically only professional printers could do. Online brokerages have made investing so inexpensive and convenient that even college students now actively manage their own portfolios. Indeed, disruptive technologies have been one of the fundamental mechanisms through which the quality of our lives has improved. In each of these cases, the disruption left consumers far better off than they had been—we don't yearn to return to the days of the corporate mainframe center, for example.

Our health care system needs to be transformed in the same way. Rather than ask complex, high-cost institutions and expensive, specialized professionals to move down-market, we need to look at the problem in a very different way. Managers and technologies need to focus instead on enabling less expensive professionals to do progressively more sophisticated things in less expensive settings.

We need diagnostic and therapeutic advances that allow nurse practitioners to treat diseases that used to require a physician's care, for example, or primary care physicians to treat conditions that used to require specialists. Similarly, we need innovations that enable procedures to be done in less expensive, more convenient settings—for doctors to provide services in their offices that used to be done during a hospital stay, for example. The graphs "Disruptions of health care professions" and "Disruptions of health care institutions" suggest the patterns by which these disruptive innovations might transform health care.

Some innovations of exactly this sort have transformed pockets of the health care system, and where they have happened, higher quality, greater convenience, and lower cost actually have been achieved. Before 1980, for example, patients with diabetes could only know whether they had abnormal levels of glucose in their blood indirectly; they used an often inaccurate

Disruptions of health care professions

As specialist physicians continue to concentrate on curing the most incurable of illnesses for the sickest of patients, less-skilled practitioners could take on more complex roles than they are currently being allowed to do. Already, a host of over-the-counter drugs allow patients to administer care that used to require a doctor's prescription. Nurse practitioners are capable of treating many ailments that used to require a physician's care. And new procedures like angioplasty are allowing cardiologists to treat patients that in the past would have needed the services of open-heart surgeons.

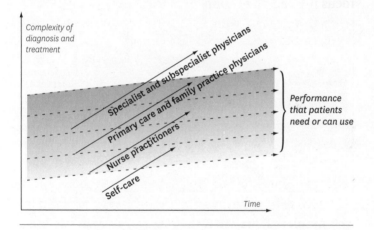

urine test or visited a doctor who drew a blood sample and then measured its glucose content on an expensive piece of laboratory equipment. Today, patients pack miniature blood glucose meters with them wherever they go; they themselves now manage most aspects of a disease that previously had required much more professional involvement. They get far higher quality care far more conveniently. No patient or professional pines

Disruptions of health care institutions

Teaching hospitals incur great costs to develop the ability to treat difficult, intractable illnesses at the high end. In the process, they have come to overserve the needs of the much larger population of patients whose disorders are becoming more and more routine. Most types of patients that occupied hospital beds 20 years ago are now being treated in more-focused care centers and outpatient clinics, doctors' offices, and even at home.

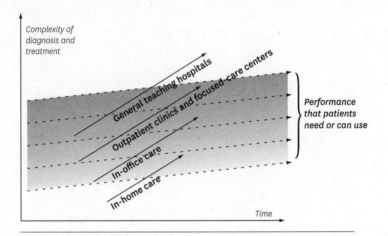

for the good old days—even though the companies that made the large laboratory blood-glucose testers were all driven from the market, and endocrinologists now face significantly reduced demand for their services.

Angioplasty is another example. Before the early 1980s, patients with coronary artery disease were treated through bypass surgery. It required a complex, technologically sophisticated surgical team, as well as multiple specialists in several disciplines, complicated equipment, days in the hospital, and weeks in recovery. The far simpler angioplasty uses a balloon to dilate narrowed arteries, causing less pain and disability. It enables less expensive or specialized practitioners to treat more people with coronary artery disease in lower cost settings. Initially, angioplasty was used in only the easiest cases and was much less effective than surgery. Experts viewed the procedure with skepticism because of all the things it and its practitioners couldn't do. But over time the disruptive innovation improved. Increasing skill and experience, together with sustaining technological innovations such as stents, have allowed angioplasty to supplant surgery in many cases. Angioplasty can now be reliably performed in stand-alone cardiac care centers, which aren't burdened with the tremendous overhead costs of hospitals.

By enabling less expensive practitioners to treat diabetes and coronary artery disease in less costly locations, these disruptive innovations have made health care more efficient. But more important, no compromises in quality were made. On the contrary, more patients get more care. When care is complex, expensive, and inconvenient, many afflictions simply go untreated. Before the disruption of angioplasty, for example, many people with coronary artery disease were not treated. Patients had to be disabled with chest pain or at risk of heart attack to justify the expense and inconvenience of open-heart surgery.

We need many more such disruptions—and today we have them within our reach. Unfortunately, the people and institutions whose livelihoods they threaten often resist them. We saw such resistance in the story of the portable X-ray machine. Here's another example. An English entrepreneur has developed a system for customizing eyeglasses quickly and efficiently. The patient puts on a pair of eyeglasses with seemingly flat lenses and an odd-looking rubber bulb attached to each stem. Looking at a vision-test chart and covering one eye, she squeezes the bulb on the right stem until she can read the fine print on the chart. A monomer in the bulb shapes the lens until that eye can see perfectly. She repeats the process for the other eye. Within two minutes, she has perfectly tailored eyeglasses—at a cost of about $5. This is a disruptive technology. It lets patients do for themselves something that historically required the skill of professionals.

Predictably, the established professions quickly mobilized to discredit the entrepreneur's technology, asserting that dangers such as glaucoma might go undetected if patients corrected their own vision and that for the long-term well-being of patients, care of the eyes must be left in the hands of professionals. Of course this is a reasonable concern. But it frames the problem incorrectly. The problem should be, instead, let's find a way to allow patients to correct vision for themselves while finding new ways for professionals to catch potentially serious disorders at an early stage.

Such resistance affects not only technology but people as well. Take nurse practitioners and physicians' assistants. Because of advances in diagnostic and therapeutic technologies, these clinicians can now competently, reliably diagnose and treat simple disorders that would have required the training and judgment of a physician only a few years ago. Accurate new tests, for example, allow physicians' assistants to diagnose diseases as simple as strep infections and as serious as diabetes. In addition, studies have shown that nurse practitioners typically devote more time to patients during consultations than physicians do and emphasize prevention and health maintenance to a greater degree.[2] But many states have regulations that prevent nurse practitioners from diagnosing diseases or from prescribing treatment that they are fully capable of handling.

The flawed rationale behind such policies is that because nurse practitioners are not as highly trained as physicians, they are not capable of providing care of comparable quality. This is the same logic that minicomputer makers used to discredit the personal computer. When a physician diagnoses a simple infectious disease, the patient uses only that fraction of the physician's training that relates to simple infectious diseases. Studies have shown that nurse practitioners with comparable training in simple infectious diseases can provide care of comparable quality in that tier of the market—even though they lack training in more complex disorders.[3]

Some nearsighted advocates of patients' rights assert that nurse practitioners might not have the judgment to recognize when a disorder is beyond their expertise. But family practice doctors recognize when they can treat a disorder and when it merits referral to a specialist. Surely nurse practitioners, working at even simpler tiers of the market, can be equipped to do the same

Patient Welfare in Disruptive Times

HOW MIGHT PATIENTS FARE AMIDST health care disruptions? The answer depends on whether competitive markets are allowed to work efficiently. If clinicians or patients are forced to use less expensive technologies, disaster will result. But if consumers and providers are given choices, the use of disruptive technologies will migrate to those applications where they create real value.

Consider Sonosite, a Seattle-area company that makes a small, highly portable, inexpensive ultrasound machine. The machine is good, but it is disruptive—it lacks the analytical features and the degree of resolution found in more expensive ultrasound equipment. If a managed care organization forced echocardiologists and OB-GYN physicians to use these less expensive devices for situations in which they previously have used traditional equipment, a specialist could risk missing something important, and the patient's well-being could be compromised. But suppose instead that because Sonosite's technology now makes ultrasound accessible and affordable to generalist clinicians, they could begin to provide better, more accurate care within the low-cost and more convenient context of their offices. Instead of conducting exams in which they hypothesize about what's going on inside a

thing. The real reason for blocking such disruption, we suspect, is the predictable desire of physicians to preserve their traditional market hegemony.

Instead of working to enable the natural upmarket migration that is an intrinsic part of economic progress, today's managed care organizations, insurers, and regulators have done just the opposite. They have forced highly trained physicians down-market to diagnose ear infections and bronchitis and have prevented nurse patient's body by listening through a stethoscope or by using their fingers to probe for irregularities, they could use this simple ultrasound device that would let them see inside the body. By enabling generalists to diagnose more quickly and with greater precision, disruptive technologies such as Sonosite's can improve, not compromise, the cost, quality, and convenience of care.

Ultimately, we would expect that the disruptive portable machines will improve to the point that they will supplant the more expensive traditional ultrasound equipment in established applications as well. But the true transformative impact of such technologies in health care will come as they allow less expensive professionals to provide better care.

If history is any guide, the established high-end providers of products and services are likely to be articulate and assertive about preserving existing systems in order to ensure patient well-being. Very often, however, their eloquence reflects concerns about their own well-being. Customers have almost always emerged from disruptive transitions better off—as long as the disruptions are not forced into an old mode, but instead enable better service to be delivered in a less-costly, more convenient context.

practitioners from doing things that technology enables them to do perfectly well. The result of this policy is perverse. To maintain their incomes, primary care physicians are forced to churn patients at an alarming rate—frequently spending only a few minutes with each patient. That reduces the quality and convenience of care.

This practice, which has become pervasive in most managed care organizations, is akin to what would have happened if some regulatory body in the early 1980s had decreed that because microprocessors were inferior in computing power to wired logic circuits, all personal computers had to be equipped with wired logic boards, not microprocessors. Such a regulation would have halted the industry's progress. The fact that we were able to use microprocessor-based computers for the jobs they were capable of handling, and wired-logic-based machines for the jobs for which microprocessors weren't suited, has been a key to the creation of high-quality, convenient, cost-effective computing for all of us. Enabling less expensive people to do things that were previously unimaginable has been one of the fundamental engines of economic progress—and the established health care institutions have fought that engine tooth and nail.

Solutions to the Crisis

The crisis in health care is deep, to be sure. But the history of other disruptive revolutions offers a number of suggestions for how a systemic transformation might be managed. We describe some of these here:

Create—Then Embrace—a System Where the Clinician's Skill Level Is Matched to the Difficulty of the Medical Problem

Medical problems range from the very simple to the very complex, as we've said. Let's look more closely at that range for a moment. In the simplest tiers, diagnosis and treatment can be rule-based: accurate data yield an unambiguous diagnosis, indicating a proven therapeutic strategy. Many infectious diseases fall into this category. In the middle tiers, diagnosis and treatment occur through pattern recognition—no single piece of data yields an answer, but multiple data points lead to a definitive diagnosis. The onset of Type I diabetes, for example, is diagnosed when a pattern is observed—blurry vision, incessant thirst, weight loss, and frequent urination. Once a diagnosis is confirmed, relatively standardized treatment protocols often exist. In the most complex disorders, diagnosis and treatment occur in a problem-solving mode. These problems require the collective experience and judgment of a team of clinical investigators and often involve cycles of testing, hypotheses, and experimentation.

By now it's clear that the simplest tiers can be reliably treated and diagnosed by less highly skilled clinicians—and also that institutional forces will fight that reality. We cannot allow such opposition to arrest reform. Instead, we must invent processes that can channel complex problems, which can't be solved in a rule-based mode, to clinicians whose skills are appropriate to a pattern-recognition or a problem-solving mode.

Scientific progress moves disorders that used to be dealt with in a problem-solving mode toward a pattern-recognition mode and those that had to be addressed through pattern recognition toward a rule-based regime. Mapping the human genome will accelerate this process. Not long ago, for example, leukemia was thought to be a single disease. Diagnosing and treating it was complex—no two patients responded identically to the same therapy, and treatment required the experience, intuition, and problem-solving skills of the best oncologists. Our improved understanding of the human genetic code, however, has helped researchers see that what we previously called leukemia is really at least six different diseases. Each is characterized by a specific genetic pattern, and patients can be precisely diagnosed by matching their patterns to a template.

Where once therapy used to be applied experimentally, such precise definition of the disease will allow for precise treatment protocols. Disruptive technologies such as this are precisely what are needed to reform health care. They will continue to enable less-experienced caregivers to make more precise diagnoses and provide higher quality care than they could have in problem-solving mode.

It's in physicians' interest to embrace this change. Rather than fight the nurse practitioners who are invading their turf, primary care physicians should move upmarket themselves, using advances in diagnostic and therapeutic technologies to perform many of the services they now refer to costly hospitals and specialists. They should, in other words, disrupt those above them rather than fight a reactionary and ultimately futile battle with disrupters from below.[4] Let us be clear. Many managed care organizations today give primary care physicians a financial incentive *not* to refer patients to specialists—to continue treating patients they are not competent to care for. Inviting them to move incompetently upmarket is a recipe for disaster. Disruptive technologies such as those we have described will enable these caregivers to move *competently* upward. These innovations are the sort that will reform health care. This strategy—unlike the one that pushes these physicians down-market or encourages them upward without enabling technology—is consistent with the way technological progress and customer needs interact.

Invest Less Money in High-End, Complex Technologies and More in Technologies That Simplify Complex Problems
Equity markets have not been generous to companies making health care products and equipment in recent years. Other sectors of the economy are perceived to exhibit greater growth and profit potential. One reason for this, we believe, is that much of the energy and capital spent in the development of new health care products and services have been targeted at the high end—at sustaining technologies that enable the most skilled practitioners to solve problems that could not be solved before. We do not contest the value of these innovations—but they will not transform health care. The great growth opportunities exist in the simpler tiers of the market. History tells us that major new growth markets coalesce when products, processes, and information technologies let less highly paid groups of people do things in more convenient settings. To truly disrupt the health care system, venture capital, entrepreneurial energy, and technology development need to flow toward these enabling initiatives. Rather than focus on complex solutions for complex problems, research and development need to focus on simplification.

It's not entirely clear why more venture capital hasn't flowed in this direction. One possible reason is that individual entrepreneurial companies don't get to pick fights with individual Goliaths—more often, they face an army of giants. Because regulators, litigators, insurers, physicians, hospitals, and medical schools have such powerful interlocking interests in the status quo, disruption might require the concerted strategic focus of major health care companies such as Johnson & Johnson, Baxter, Medtronic, or Merck. Over time, they could overcome the inertia of entrenched institutions. A series of disruptive business ventures launched by these companies would create far greater growth for them, with less investment, than would continued pursuit of sustaining technologies that enable specialists to push further into high-end complexities.

Create New Organizations to Do the Disrupting

The health care industry today is trying to preserve outmoded institutions. Yet the history of disruptive innovations tells us that those institutions will be replaced, soon enough, with new institutions whose business models are appropriate to the new technologies and markets.

When disruptive innovations have invaded the mainstream markets of other industries, a difficult period typically has preceded the arrival of truly convenient, lower cost, higher quality products and services. Between 1988 and 1993, for example, as networked personal computers became the dominant information technology architecture, the former industry leaders fell into disarray.

Together, the mainframe and minicomputer makers logged $20 billion in operating losses during that period. None of these companies was able to adapt its business model to compete in the personal computer world. Instead, they seemed able only to tighten the thumbscrews on their existing processes, attacking costs through mergers and layoffs, as they withered away. During this period, it wasn't the computer industry that was in crisis—only its traditional institutions were. Disruptive innovators such as Intel, Sun, Microsoft, and Dell were creating extraordinary value.

The massive financial losses that hospitals and managed care institutions are suffering today mirror exactly what happened to the dominant players in other disrupted industries. And they are responding in the same way—by tightening controls on their existing business models. They are merging, closing facilities, laying off workers, forming buying groups, delaying payments, adding layers of control-oriented overhead workers, and hiring consultants—while going about their work in a fundamentally unchanged way. In fact, the billions of dollars large general hospitals are spending to build information technology systems and to create integrated feeder systems of physicians' group practices and primary-, secondary-, and tertiary-care hospitals are designed to preserve, rather than displace, the existing institutions.

We will always need some general hospitals to provide intensive and critical care to the sickest patients, just as we still need IBM and Hitachi to make mainframe computers for the most complex computing applications.

But it is very likely that the care of disorders that primarily involve one system in the body—from earaches to cardiac and renal illnesses—will migrate to focused institutions whose scope enables them to provide better care with less complexity-driven overhead. If history is any guide, the health care system can be transformed only by creating new institutions that can capably deliver the vast majority of such care, rather than attempting a tortuous transformation of existing institutions that were designed for other purposes.

Leaders of today's hospital and managed care companies might profit from comparing the approaches that S.S. Kresge and F.W. Woolworth took toward disruptive discount retailing, beginning in the early 1960s, as recounted in Clayton Christensen's *The Innovator's Dilemma*. Kresge addressed the disruption by systematically closing 10% of its variety stores every year and funneling all its cash into its disruptive start-up, Kmart. Woolworth, by contrast, tried to maintain its pace of investment in its traditional stores while building its discount-retailing arm, Woolco. Despite the fact that Woolworth was far larger and had much deeper pockets, Woolco—and ultimately all of Woolworth's variety stores—folded. The lessons for today's medical institutions: don't be scared to invent the institution that could put you out of business, and stop investing in dying business models.

Overcome the Inertia of Regulation

Attempts to use regulation to stave off disruptive attacks are quite common. The U.S. automakers, for example, relied on import quotas as long as they could to keep disruptive Toyota and Honda at bay. Unfortunately, regulators are inclined to be even more protective of the entrenched professions and institutions in health care than they were of the U.S. automakers. The links between those institutions, federal and state regulators, and insurance companies are strong; they are wielded to preserve the status quo. (Nothing else could explain why nurse practitioners are forbidden from diagnosing simple illnesses in so many states.)

Instead of working to preserve the existing system, regulators need to frame their jobs differently. They need to ask how they can enable disruptive innovations to emerge. Let's return to the example we began with—the low-cost X-ray machine. Suppose the regulators wanted to see this disruptive innovation work in doctors' offices but were concerned about potential risks. They might require that all images interpreted in a physician's office by a nonradiologist be transmitted via the Internet to a second-opinion center, where skilled radiologists could confirm those initial diagnoses. Admittedly, that would require a massive change in the way regulators do their work.

The Need for Leadership

Once an industry is in crisis, individual leaders often become paralyzed. They're incapable of embracing disruptive approaches because the profitability of the institutions they lead has been so eroded. Typically, not only do they ignore the potential disruptions, they actively work to discredit and oppose them. Thus far, this pattern has held true in the health care industry as well.

Successful disruptive revolution of this system will unfold more quickly, and far less painfully for everyone, if leaders at regional and national levels work together—not to regulate the existing system but to coordinate the removal of the barriers that have prevented disruptions from happening. Unfortunately, in this presidential election year, the proposals from both leading parties for dealing with the crisis in health care have been molded within the established system. These proposals can be divided into three categories of solutions: control costs by consuming less health care; impose reimbursement controls that force high-end providers to become more efficient; and use government money to subsidize the high costs of health care for targeted segments of the population. None of these proposals addresses the fundamental causes of the dilemmas that the health care system faces.

Government and health care industry leaders need to step forward—to help insurers, regulators, managed care organizations, hospitals, and health professionals work together to facilitate disruption instead of uniting to prevent it. If they do, some of the established institutions will fail. But many more health care providers will realize the opportunities for growth that come with disruption—because disruption is the fundamental mechanism through which we will build a higher quality, more convenient, and lower cost health care system. If leaders with such vision do indeed step forward, we will all have access to more health care, not less.

Notes

The authors express appreciation to Jeff Elton and his staff at Integral, Incorporated for their contributions to this article.

1. Clayton M. Christensen, The Innovator's Dilemma: When New Technologies Cause Great Firms to Fail (Harvard Business School Press, 1997).

2. See James Lardner, "For Nurses, a Barrier Is Broken," *U.S. News & World Report,* July 1998.

3. Richard A. Cooper, MD, et al. "Roles of Non-physician Clinicians as Autonomous Providers of Patient Care," *JAMA,* September 2, 1998. These market forces are already at work. It is estimated that by the year 2005, the number of nurse practitioners in clinical practice will equal the number of family physicians. Between 1992 and 1997, the number of schools offering qualification programs for NPs more than doubled, from less than 100 to approximately 250. During that same time, the number of students pursuing NP degrees quintupled, from 4,000 to over 20,000.

4. Evidence that specialists are already being disrupted in this manner can be found in a 1995 report by the Council of Graduate Medical Education, which predicted an excess of 115,000 specialists by the year 2000. See Stephen M. Shortell et al., *Remaking Health Care in America: Building Organized Delivery Systems* (Jossey-Bass Publishers, 1996), p. 298.

CLAYTON M. CHRISTENSEN is a professor of business administration at Harvard Business School. **RICHARD M.J. BOHMER** is a physician and a senior lecturer at Harvard Business School. **JOHN KENAGY** is a physician and a clinical associate professor of surgery at the University of Washington in Seattle.

Originally published in September 2000. Reprint 6972

Saving Money,
Saving Lives

by Jon Meliones

MY EPIPHANY CAME AT SEVEN O'CLOCK on a hectic November evening in 1996. I was the attending physician in the intensive care unit at Duke Children's Hospital (DCH) in Durham, North Carolina. A six-month-old named Alex lay in a crib in the ICU with a stiff plastic tube in her throat. Awake and moving after heart surgery, the tiny girl was ready to come off the ventilator. As Alex squirmed and tried to breathe, the ventilator forced more air into her lungs. Her exhausted parents grew distraught. "Why can't she come off the ventilator?" her mother asked. "Because we've had to cut back on night staff," replied the busy nurse. "There's no respiratory therapist available." Alex was uncomfortable. She received medication to help her sleep and to keep her from fighting the ventilator until the therapist arrived in the morning. But her parents didn't sleep; they were too confused and upset.

As I watched Alex and her parents, I thought back to similar scenes I had witnessed over the years at DCH, a

134-bed pediatric hospital located on the fifth floor of Duke University Hospital. Here, 800 employees care for patients in our neonatal intensive care unit, pediatric intensive care unit and pediatric emergency room, bone-marrow transplant and intermediate care units, as well as in our subspecialty and outreach clinics. When I came to DCH in 1992, we had a $4 million annual operating loss; it had grown to $11 million by 1996, which forced administrators to cut back on resources. As a result, some caregivers felt that the quality of clinical care had deteriorated. Parents' complaints increased. Some dissatisfied doctors threatened to send their patients elsewhere. Frustrated staff quit.

And then it struck me. I saw with perfect clarity the reason that DCH was struggling to meet the needs of its customers—our patients and their parents. And I knew what had to be done to make things right. The problem was that our hospital was a collection of fiefdoms: each group, from accountants to administrators to clinicians, was focusing on its individual goal rather than on the organization as a whole. We would be a far more effective organization if we could stop that from happening. Most companies in the United States had this insight companies 20 years ago, but the nonprofit world remains, for the most part, unaware of it. I realized that DCH needed to start thinking less like a money-losing nonprofit and more like a profitable corporation.

A sense of mission, of course, is critical to any organization's identity. The institutional mission of a hospital is to promote the health of the community. But during difficult periods, it's easy to lose sight of the big

Idea in Brief

In 1996, Duke Children's Hospital was in serious trouble. Its $11 million annual operating loss had forced administrators to make cutbacks. As a result, some caregivers felt that the quality of care had deteriorated. Parents' complaints were on the rise. Frustrated staff members were quitting. In this article, Jon Meliones, DCH's chief medical director, candidly describes how his debt-ridden hospital transformed itself into a vibrant and profitable one. The problem, he realized, was that each group in DCH was focusing only on its individual mission. Doctors and nurses wanted to restore their patients to health; they didn't want to have to think about costs. Hospital administrators, for their part, were focused only on controlling wildly escalating health care costs. To keep DCH afloat, clinicians and administrators needed to work together. By listening to staff concerns, turning reams of confusing data into useful information, taking a fresh approach to teamwork, and using the balanced scorecard method, Meliones and his colleagues brought DCH back to life. This first-person account is required reading for any executive seeking to revitalize a sagging organization. Meliones shares the operating principles DCH followed to become a thriving business.

picture and focus solely on your fiefdom's specific goals. Clinicians—that is, doctors and nurses—want to restore their patients to health; they don't want to think about costs. Hospital administrators have their own mission—to control wildly escalating health care costs.

Cost cutting in a vacuum traumatizes patients, frustrates clinicians, and ultimately cripples the hospital's mission. The decision to cut a respiratory therapist from the night shift, for example, affected Alex and her parents as well as their insurance company, which had to pay an additional $2,000 to cover the cost of the ventilator and ICU care. The decision also left the clinicians feeling powerless, since decisions regarding clinical practice were being made without their input. Such trade-offs between quality of patient care and cost control cause intense conflict for health care professionals. In worst-case situations, efforts to improve profit margins actually have the opposite effect—they chase away customers, cost executives their jobs, and put the entire hospital at risk of financial ruin.

Regaining Our Balance

Considering the magnitude of the issues we faced—a $7 million increase in annual losses in four years—it's hard to believe that we ever turned things around. But we did, by changing people's minds and hearts, inch by inch, day by day. In 1997, the chief nurse executive, nurse managers, and I began working together to start turning the organization around. First, we discussed our current realities with the entire clinical team. We opened the meetings by talking about our goals for our patients. "We want patients to be happy," the doctors and nurses agreed, "and for them to have the best care." We also described our pressing financial challenges.

We showed the clinicians our raw data. The average length of stay at DCH was eight days— 20% longer than the six-day national average. The average per-patient cost was $15,000—more money than we were bringing in. If we continued to spend at the same rates, we would be forced to cut clinical programs, staff, and beds. The quality of patient care and our reputation would then suffer, and we would fail to meet the needs of our community.

Confronted with this grim picture, the clinicians began to understand that if we wanted to save our programs and our patients, create an environment in which staff are fulfilled, and keep our jobs, we would all have to readjust our individual missions and start paying attention to costs. If the hospital didn't show a margin, clinicians wouldn't be able to fulfill their mission. Thus, we adopted the now-familiar mantra in health care: no margin, no mission.

It was also clear that the administrators needed to be highly involved. To bring the administrators' and the clinician's missions into alignment, we turned to a practical management approach that had worked well in numerous *Fortune* 500 corporations: the balanced scorecard method. Developed by Robert Kaplan and David Norton, it had improved customer service, driven organizational change, and boosted bottom-line performance in leading companies like AT&T, Intel, and 3M. Our goal was to become the health care leader in the balanced scorecard.

Our balanced scorecard aligned the hospital's goals along four equally important quadrants: financial health; customer satisfaction; internal business procedures; and employee satisfaction. We explained the theory to clinicians and administrators like this: if you sacrifice too much in one quadrant to satisfy another, your organization as a whole is thrown out of balance. We could, for example, cut costs to improve the financial quadrant by firing half the staff, but that would hurt quality of service, and the customer quadrant would fall out of balance. Or we could increase productivity in the internal business quadrant by assigning more patients to a nurse, but doing so would raise the likelihood of errors—an unacceptable trade-off. Our vision, which became the new mission statement, was to provide patients and families with high quality, compassionate care within an efficient organization.

Taking Our Medicine

Developing and implementing a balanced scorecard in labor intensive because it is a consensus-driven methodology. To make ours work required nothing short of a pilot project, a top-down reorganization, development of a customized information system, and systematic work redesign. The most difficult challenge was convincing employees that they must work in different ways.

At first, doctors and managers saw attempts to move them into teams as a shift in their power base. Nearly everyone complained that applying a systematic approach to cost management was "cookbook medicine." It took a good deal of persuasion, persistence, and reassurance to get some individuals to buy into our process. One cardiologist routinely stormed out of meetings when we talked about cost per case.

We knew that changing people's minds would be hard work. But once people saw how successful the balanced scorecard approach was in one area of the hospital, we reasoned, it would be easier to sell the

A look at the numbers

Using the balanced scorecard method, Duke Children's Hospital's cost-per-case average fell from nearly $15,000 to $10,500 and its margin soared from an $11 million annual loss to a $4 million gain.

Cost per case

$14,889

$13,411

$12,550 $12,440

$10,500

1996   1997   1998   1999   2000

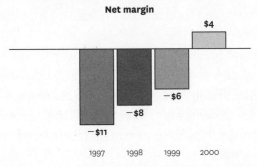

Net margin

$4

−$6

−$8

−$11

1997   1998   1999   2000

methodology throughout the rest of the organization. So we decided to launch a pilot project. Some physicians were much more willing to change than others. Those who understood the importance of applying systems to medicine—such as surgeons—became our first champions. So we started the balanced scorecard in one very important microcosm of the hospital—the pediatric intensive care unit, which I lead.

First, we reorganized the roles that individuals play in the ICU. We moved from mission-bound departments in which people identified only with their particular jobs ("I am a manager," "I am a nurse," and so on) to goal-oriented, multidisciplinary teams focused on a particular illness or disease ("We, the ICU team, consisting of the manager, the nurse, the physician, the pharmacist, and the radiologist, help children with heart problems"). We called these teams clinical business units—what other industries call business or operating units. The lead physician and the lead administrator shared responsibility in these teams. Together, they reviewed financial information, patient and staff satisfaction data, and information on health care trends and initiatives.

The various clinical business units worked together to organize "care coordination rounds" and brainstorm solutions to difficult patient cases. They created a patient's care plan—a document, shared with the parents, that records everything from treatment recommendations to post-hospital care.

The teams also developed protocols we call clinical pathways—a set of best practices for various treatments. For example, a respiratory therapist, a nurse, and a physician developed a series of steps a nurse could follow to remove a patient from a respirator without having a therapist present. As the clinicians developed new pathways, they shared their successes with the entire organization so we could all learn from their experience.

By developing and promoting protocols like these, we improved care dramatically. For example, we knew that babies recovering from heart surgery had trouble feeding and that parents needed to learn how to help them. Before we had formed the pathways, we would wait until the day of discharge to teach parents how to do so. Once people started sharing their expertise to develop the pathways, we learned that there was no reason to wait so long and moved the training to the day after surgery. Patients were able to go home much sooner, and their hospital costs were cut by 28%.

We developed more protocols by comparing patient data. A study of 20 heart patients, for example, revealed that treatment costs varied dramatically. One child received two days' worth of antibiotics; another received seven days' worth for the same condition. One child underwent ten laboratory tests; another had only three, and so on. As a group, the clinicians went over each case, comparing notes and reviewing the medical literature. They decided which tests were unnecessary and eliminated them.

Within six months, our balanced scorecard approach in the ICU was garnering impressive results. We reduced the cost per case by nearly 12% and improved our measured patient satisfaction by 8%. In fact, our pilot project was working so well that we implemented it in pediatrics, then in all of the other areas of DCH, within a year. We didn't use a cookie-cutter approach; rather, leaders in each unit customized the scorecard template for their specific areas.

Over time, even the physician who had angrily left our initial meetings began to find ways to lower his cost per case without compromising patient care. For example, instead of keeping some patients awaiting surgery in the hospital, he discharged them overnight to a nearby hotel, lowering the total cost by $1,000 per day while making the patients and their parents much more comfortable.

A Measure of Progress

Like most hospitals, DCH collects a tremendous amount of data. We rigorously detail things like length of stay, number of staff, cost per case, and so on. But we were culling very little useful information from the data—and some of it was false. For example, the first report card on my own performance showed that I had discharged 70 patients with an average length of stay of 29 days and an average cost per case of $70,000. Taken together, these numbers deserved a grade of F. I knew that since I'd been head of the intensive care unit, I'd cared for and transferred 1,500 patients. What was going on here? A closer look at the data revealed that they reported on only the 70 patients who had died, not my total caseload.

Clearly, we needed to approach the data in a new way and turn it into useful information. Unless we did, we wouldn't know where our potential cost savings were. We didn't know, for example, that babies were needlessly kept on $2,000 ventilators at night, nor did we know how much that decision was costing the hospital. So for every clinical business unit, we created a measurement system for each of the four balanced scorecard quadrants.

To measure our progress, we asked our IT department to help us develop our own database and cost-accounting system. Using information pulled from national databases, we determined national average for indicators such as length of stay and complication rates. (In 1997, custom development was our only option. We've since installed StrategicVision software from SAS to support our extensive data management, trend analysis, and performance reporting needs.) The system logged each patient's treatment history and costs for everything from a $15 hypodermic needle to a $5,000 heart-lung bypass operation. The system also tracked the average waiting times for admission and discharge, blood culture contamination rates, and so on.

The new system helped us find ways to improve our performance in each of the four quadrants. Many of the steps we took were small, but cumulatively, they made a big difference. For example, our clinical pathways included a "patient care guide" for parents that explained in lay terms what they could expect to happen on a daily basis during their child's hospital stay. We also learned from our customer surveys that parents felt frustrated by not knowing who their child's attending physician or nurse was at any given time. So we simply put identification cards on the doors, naming the attending doctor and primary nurse. Our customer satisfaction scores rose sharply.

We made other changes, too. For the financial quadrant, for example, we reviewed the most significant data points, such as the number of patients admitted, treated, and released, and the cost per patient. The clinical business units reviewed cases of patients whose diagnostic, surgical, pharmacy, and postoperation costs had been the highest, and tried to determine why. In many cases, our research showed us new ways to do business. For example, we learned that children often stayed longer than necessary in our $1,700-per-day ICU, in which the nurse to patient ratio is 1 to 1 or 1 to 2. That was because the patients weren't quite ready to move to the regular pediatric floor, where the ratio of nurses to patients is 1 to 5 and the cost is $700 per day. So we created a six-bed, $1,200-per-day transitional care unit, where the nurse to patient ratio is 1 to 3. Patients could stay there until they could be moved to the general floor. Not only did our cost-per-patient numbers drop but also our patients' families got to spend more time with their recovering children.

Overall, the results we've achieved at DCH by using the balanced scorecard have been stunning. By increasing the number of clinical pathways and communicating more with parents, our customer satisfaction ratings jumped by 18%. Improvements to our internal business processes reduced the average length of stay from 7.9 days in 1996 to 6.1 days in fiscal year 2000, while the readmission rate fell from 7% to 3%. And employees noted a 45% increase in satisfaction with children's services and with the way the entire administrative team performed its job.

Impressive results occurred on the financial front, too. The cost per patient dropped by nearly $5,000—a fact not lost on parents, insurers, and our own senior leaders. By FY 2000, we had gone from $11 million in losses to profits of $4 million, even though we were admitting more patients. We achieved a reduction in costs of $29 million over these four years, without staff cutbacks. Our methodology has proved so successful that the entire Duke University Hospital now uses it as a framework. With the balanced scorecard we have drastically improved our margin and achieved our hospital's mission.

Lessons Learned

Yes, DCH has navigated a tremendous turnaround, but I don't want to suggest that it's been easy. Adopting the balanced scorecard approach presented us with huge management challenges on a daily basis. In the early stages, we often found it difficult to keep discussions on target. We spent nearly a month debating whether a certain goal or target belonged in the internal business process quadrant or the customer satisfaction quadrant. We learned to limit those discussions—it was too easy to get embroiled in semantics and lose our focus on patients and staff.

We also found that people became demoralized if we compared their performance to an abstract or too-lofty target. For that reason, we encouraged employees to

Survival Strategies

The challenges faced by Duke Children's Hospital are by no means unique to the health care industry. Indeed, many organizations find themselves in similar situations. They fear that focusing on costs will compromise their higher mission of serving the community—but in fact, a strong bottom line will make fulfilling their missions that much easier. If you're trying to turn your organization around, you may want to adopt the operating principles we followed to make DCH a thriving business.

Communicate, Communicate, Communicate

- If your organization is in trouble, be honest. Make it absolutely clear to everyone in the company that survival depends on cost management.

- Listen to what employees are saying; they know their jobs better than you do. Instead of issuing orders, ask them, "What can we (as an organization) do?"

- Share the pulpit. People with other expertise can help build consensus.

- Change people's roles; instead of identifying with an individual job ("I am a nurse"), employees should identify with goal-oriented teams ("We, the ICU team, work together to help children with heart problems").

- Offer constant feedback. Frequent evaluations help keep the organization on track.

---

use their own performance as the primary benchmark. Still, if they wanted to see how their performance compared with the hospital as a whole, or with a national average, they could review those data points as well.

We learned to set our targets conservatively at first: an annual 10% reduction in the length of stay was

- Publicly celebrate every employee and team success.
- Cultivate your sense of humor—people will respond if you can laugh at yourself.

Chart Your Path

- Start with a pilot project; succeeding in one department will pave the way for organizationwide change.
- Set conservative goals at first; you'll gain the confidence needed to set more aggressive targets.
- Focus on a few key goals; changing everything at once leads to failure.
- Turn data into information. Work with your information technology people to ensure that employees can correctly interpret measurements and statistics.
- Let employees compete with their own performance, not with some abstract competitive or statistical target.

Never Stop

- When mapping your business to the balanced scorecard, don't get sidetracked by semantics.
- Be willing to experiment; learn from failures.
- Constantly revise and improve practices.
- Encourage strategic thinking at all levels.

something most of us felt comfortable reaching for, but a goal of 20% would have been too intimidating. As we became more successful, we set more aggressive targets.

And I learned that there's a fine art to communicating with professionals who know more than you do about their particular subject and who are passionate about their work. You can't just order them around. You have to get inside their heads and figure out what they're going through.

Before 1996, I thought I was a decent communicator. But over time, I've had to learn to listen carefully not only to what people are telling me but also to what I'm saying to them. Today I know that I can't make a point in a conversation by talking in the abstract. I have to say something that personally matters to the other individual. I learned not to say things like, "Duke Children's Hospital is losing $11 million per year." Rather, I opened conversations with a question, such as "How important do you think it is to have a therapist on this unit to work with your patients?" When they said it was important, I'd follow up with "How can we work together to manage our costs so we can preserve the therapist's job?"

I learned that little things make a big difference when it comes to morale building. We created all kinds of communication and feedback mechanisms. I started a newsletter, "Practicing Smarter," so staff members could share best practices and keep one another apprised of their progress. We honored "team members of the month," started on-line discussion groups, and sponsored a series of staff brown-bag lunches and open forums. These approaches may sound simple, but they really did help to change our culture. For the first time, employees felt that their opinions mattered.

I discovered how important it is to share the pulpit during dramatic organizational changes. Not only did I respect the chief nurse executive, the managers, and the administrators as partners, but I knew that they could communicate more effectively with their own constituencies than I ever could.

Even in the most earnest conversations, I've found that having a sense of humor is essential. For example, I developed a Letterman-style list of the "Top Ten Reasons for Using the Balanced Scorecard," poking fun at myself in meetings. Once, I even walked through the hospital dressed up as the eminently poke-able Pillsbury Doughboy. Keeping things light made it easier for us all to endure the tremendously challenging course we'd set for ourselves.

I learned, too, to respect the persuasive power of meaningful information. I spent hours with members of our IT department, telling them what the staff was telling me—trying to slice and dice our enormous mountains of data into useful information. When we finally presented people with accurate tracking measures about their personal performance, they were fascinated—and anxious to improve.

It's been four years since we set out to improve performance at Duke Children's Hospital, and changes are still happening. We talk about our scorecard constantly; we're fine-tuning what works and discarding what doesn't. Whenever a clinician comes up with a better pathway, we spread the word through our newsletter and on our bulletin boards.

Of all the changes that have occurred, the most telling are the ones we see in our patients. Consider the case of Ryan, a four-month-old who recently recovered from heart surgery. At 8 PM, Ryan was breathing with a ventilator—just as Alex had—and his parents kept vigil by his crib. But unlike Alex's parents, Ryan's parents knew exactly who was responsible for their child's care, what his care entailed, and that he'd soon be transferred to an intermediate care unit. At 9 PM, Ryan began breathing on his own. The nurse skillfully removed the plastic tube and gently placed him on his mother's lap. For me, seeing Ryan sleeping peacefully in his mother's arms was a rewarding end to a long, hard, but ultimately satisfying journey.

JON MELIONES, MD, is the chief medical director at Duke Children's Hospital in North Carolina and a professor of pediatrics and anesthesia at Duke University Medical Center.

Originally published in November 2000. Reprint R00612

Rebuilding the R&D Engine in Big Pharma

by Jean-Pierre Garnier

HISTORICALLY, THE PHARMACEUTICAL INDUSTRY has been a leader in financial performance and value creation. In recent years, however, its stock-market record has raised doubts about the sustainability of that history along with fundamental questions about the industry's health. From December 2000 to February 2008 the top 15 companies in the industry lost roughly $850 billion in shareholder value, and the price of their shares fell from 32 times earnings, on average, to 13.

The common explanation for investors' loss of faith is the well-known perfect storm of trends—pricing pressures, regulatory requirements, legal entanglements, inroads by generics, and declining R&D productivity—that have increased the industry's costs enormously and reduced its revenue and profit potential. I certainly agree that all of these trends are problems for the industry. But I believe that declining R&D productivity is at the center of its malaise.

Some critics question whether so-called Big Pharma can fix its R&D engine. They predict that more-nimble new enterprises like those in the biotech sector will supplant the lumbering dinosaurs. I strongly disagree. There are benefits to size: It provides the critical mass

From leaders to laggards

The graph below compares the average annual return to shareholders (stock appreciation plus dividends) of various industries, weighted by market capitalization and expressed in percentages. The pharmaceutical industry's significant lead in creating shareholder value evaporated between the two time periods shown. This occurred even though the industry's gross and EBITDA margins rose steadily for 20 years—to 78% and 32%, respectively, in 2005.

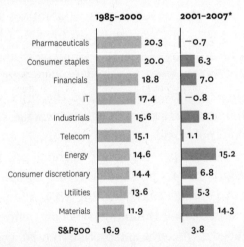

	1985–2000	2001–2007*
Pharmaceuticals	20.3	−0.7
Consumer staples	20.0	6.3
Financials	18.8	7.0
IT	17.4	−0.8
Industrials	15.6	8.1
Telecom	15.1	1.1
Energy	14.6	15.2
Consumer discretionary	14.4	6.8
Utilities	13.6	5.3
Materials	11.9	14.3
S&P500	16.9	3.8

*Data as of June 30, 2007. All U.S. publicly traded companies with revenues of $500M or more, adjusted for inflation.

Idea in Brief

From December 2000 to February 2008, the top 15 companies in the pharmaceutical industry lost roughly $850 billion in shareholder value. Although a number of factors—including the rise of generics, pricing pressures, regulatory requirements, and legal entanglements—are to blame, Garnier, the CEO of GlaxoSmith Kline, believes that declining R&D productivity is his industry's primary problem. The way to solve it, he says, is to return power to the scientists—by reorganizing R&D into highly focused groups headed by inspirational leaders, seeking the best science outside as well as inside a company, fixing broken processes, and promoting a strong culture of innovation and passion for excellence. GSK has replaced its organizational pyramid with 12 "centers of excellence." The company has worked to untangle the quest for breakthrough drugs from the effort to develop best-in-class offerings and has overhauled incentives

for the scientists who actually make discoveries. It has also pursued contractual relationships with academia and biotech companies in a bid to secure the best science, wherever it may reside. When the company began a sweeping reengineering of its R&D, it had only two products in late-stage development. Today it has 34—the most in the industry. But much more remains to be done, the author says. Significant cost efficiencies could be achieved by offshoring clinical trials. Development of new blockbuster drugs could be simplified and accelerated if researchers targeted only a limited segment of the potential patient population and then expanded to others over time. The innovation malaise in pharmaceuticals is not unique, Garnier says. Many other industries face the same challenges. A cultural revolution and a broad transformation of the organization are necessary first steps to rebuilding the R&D engine.

needed for global clinical development and acquiring crucial technology platforms.

The way to solve the productivity problem is not to break up the pharmaceutical giants into smaller companies. It is to return power to the scientists by reorganizing

R&D into small, highly focused groups headed by people who are leaders in their scientific fields and can guide and inspire their teams to achieve greatness. It is to seek the best science wherever it resides, inside or outside a company. It is to fix broken processes and promote a strong culture of innovation marked by a passion for excellence and an awareness that results matter. The basic philosophy for modern R&D should be to morph *big* into *small* in recognition of the fact that critical mass in fundamental research is the size of one human brain.

We have been striving to do all these things at Glaxo-SmithKline since 2000, when we began a sweeping reengineering of R&D. Our results to date suggest that we are on the right track. When we began our effort, the company had only two products in late-stage development—one of the smallest numbers in the industry—despite a decade of high R&D spending. Today we have 34 drugs and vaccines—the largest number in the industry, according to Cowen equity research. A study by CMR International, a respected pharmaceutical R&D benchmarking agency, compared eight Big Pharma players on key R&D metrics (pipeline fill and flow); it shows that our productivity is now two or three times as high as the average of our competitors.

Some of the unique actions we have taken in the past eight years have already proved their value. The most significant is the breakup of our formerly mammoth R&D organization into small cross-disciplinary groups, each of which is focused on a family of related diseases. Other potentially transformational initiatives are still works in progress. Our effort to untangle the process for pursuing breakthrough therapies from that used to develop the best medicine in an already-discovered class of drugs is the most noteworthy.

This article focuses on the pharmaceutical industry. But I think many if not all of the lessons we have learned are applicable to other industries whose long-term survival depends on true breakthrough discoveries, not just incremental improvements.

The Crux of the Problem

The business model of Big Pharma is straightforward. New products are discovered, developed, launched, and protected by various patents. Initially the products benefit from monopolistic—or at least oligopolistic—pricing. After 10 or 12 years, in general, patents expire and lower-priced generics come in, wiping out the revenues of blockbuster drugs in a matter of weeks. R&D must continually replace older products with new ones to stop the revenue base from shrinking. The problem, of course, is that doing this has proved increasingly difficult.

The decrease in the pharmaceutical industry's R&D productivity—as measured by the average R&D cost per new approved drug, which includes the amount spent on failures—has been fully documented. Although the industry's collective investment in R&D from 1980 to 2006 mushroomed from $2 billion to $43 billion, the number of drugs approved by the FDA in 1980 and in 2006 was roughly the same.

One consequence of the slide in R&D productivity is the alarming decline in average *sales exclusivity:* the

An Old Model Under Attack

BIG PHARMA'S P&L STRUCTURE has long been heavily weighted toward sales and promotion and, to a lesser extent, R&D. Until the 1980s this model was extremely successful. The industry's revenues soared, and its profit margins and total return to shareholders were among the highest relative to other industries. Since the early 1990s, however, its world has dramatically changed, threatening that model.

Shorter product monopolies have fueled marketing wars.

As companies expanded their research capabilities and raced to move into any promising new opportunity that emerged, the duration of product monopolies within a given therapeutic class shrank from several years in the 1970s (for, say, Tagamet, an H2-receptor antagonist for treating gastric ailments) to a few months in the 1990s (for, say, saquinavir, a protease inhibitor for treating HIV). This trend intensified marketing wars and led to enormous sales forces. Rule changes in 1997 that allowed companies to broadcast advertising in the United States only escalated the battle. In 2006 the top seven pharmaceutical companies spent twice as much on SG&A (about 33% of revenues) as on R&D (about 16% of revenues).

A slowdown in new-product introductions has left companies with oversize sales and marketing machines.

Starting in the 1980s, R&D productivity (as measured by the average cost of discovering and developing new drugs) steadily declined. Meanwhile, the number of new blockbuster drugs (those with annual global sales of $500 million to $1 billion) has diminished. Some major drug companies have trimmed their sales and marketing functions or consolidated them in mergers, but at most companies these functions are still too large relative to the products they have to sell.

Pricing pressure is increasing globally.

Private and public payers around the world are willing to spend a lot more for truly innovative medicines: Daily treatment reimbursement rates for the new generation of oncology drugs are nearly a thousand times as high as for past oncology treatments. But such drugs are a tiny minority.

Developed countries lack a standardized system for determining the value of new products or line extensions that offer incremental or hard-to-discern improvements, making it difficult for pharmaceutical companies to win price increases for such products. Their success has heavily depended on the type of product (new category versus multiple competitors), the status of a country's health care budget, and ancillary factors such as R&D and manufacturing investments.

Overall, U.S. prices continue to surge ahead of those in developed countries with single-payer systems, and developed countries pay more, on average, than emerging or poor nations. A few pharmaceutical companies, including GlaxoSmithKline, now take a country's standard of living into account when setting prices. They charge higher prices in the United States, Europe, and Japan; intermediate prices in developing countries; and not-for-profit prices in poor countries (as defined by the United Nations). Chances are good that pricing pressure will only increase.

Revenues plunge when patents expire.

Until the mid-1980s the revenues of branded drugs declined gradually after their patents expired. No longer: A U.S. law requiring pharmacists to substitute generic versions of drugs when available, together with pressure on consumers from payers to buy lower-cost generics that differ somewhat from branded drugs, has accelerated a shift to generics. As a result, the soft landing for branded drugs has disappeared. Today multibillion-dollar blockbusters lose 90% of their revenues and profits within a few weeks of losing their patent protection.

Meanwhile, with generics the benchmark, payers are less and less willing to reimburse for line extensions at a premium. This has

(continued)

An Old Model Under Attack (continued)

made it tough for pharmaceutical companies to extend the life cycle of existing medicines.

All costs are continuing to climb.

Various third-party studies have assessed the cost of discovering and developing one new product at more than $1 billion—a dramatic increase from less than $100 million 15 years ago. Significant factors include regulatory requirements; larger, more complex clinical trials; the growing public debate about drug safety; and lawsuits.

Trends that will significantly increase demand for innovative drugs over the long term won't have a major impact on overall global volume anytime soon.

Developed nations will continue to consume innovative medicines, albeit at a slower pace. But generics now account for 70% of all prescriptions dispensed in the United States, and will continue to gain market share as multiple blockbusters lose their patent protection.

Several trends will ultimately provide a major opportunity for the pharmaceutical industry, but their impact on total global demand for branded drugs will be gradual. They include:

- *Demand from emerging economies.* Countries with high standards of living that collectively make up less than 20% of the world population (the United States, European nations, Japan) now account for 80% of the industry's global revenues and profits. This will change as rapidly developing countries such as China, India, Turkey, Russia, and Vietnam gain economic power and gradually improve their health care systems.

- *Aging populations.* The number of Alzheimer's patients in the United States, for example, is expected to grow from 5 million to 20 million within 30 years.

- *New diseases.* Although impossible to predict, the surfacing of new diseases comparable to AIDS and avian flu will trigger demand for new therapies.

remaining period of time drugs will be protected from competition by patents. Since 1999 the average exclusivity of patent-protected drugs (weighted by sales) has declined from five and a half years to less than four, the lowest level ever. A number of blockbuster drugs will lose their monopolies within the next four years, making it a watershed period for the industry.

A variety of forces are collectively responsible for the drop in the number of blockbuster drugs launched every year and the overall slide in R&D productivity. Those commonly cited include tougher challenges (the diseases easiest to treat or cure have been tackled), greater regulatory requirements, and the skyrocketing costs of every aspect of R&D, from producing a case report on a patient in a clinical trial to building a chemical pilot plant. Discovering and developing a new medicine takes at least 12 years, and the average cost is now more than $1 billion—higher than NASA's budget for sending a rocket to the moon. (See the sidebar "An Old Model Under Attack.")

Another culprit is the enormous size and complexity of the traditional pharmaceutical R&D organization. In drugs, electronics, software, and other industries where fundamental discovery (as opposed to continuous improvement) is the key to success, size has become an impediment. Two classic company examples are Bell Labs and IBM, which in their heyday innovated and won recognition again and again. Then, for a variety of reasons—most of them rooted in increasing size and bureaucratization—they stopped being the true innovators, the breakthrough discoverers. Top scientists with a low tolerance for bureaucracy left; with no clear mission, those who stayed often aimlessly pursued their own interests.

If not creatively managed, complexity can cause passionate engagement and courageous risk taking to give way to risk aversion, promises with no obligation to deliver, and bureaucratic inertia. To make matters worse, the leaders of major corporations in some industries, including pharmaceuticals and electronics, have incorrectly assumed that R&D was scalable, could be industrialized, and could be driven by detailed metrics (scorecards) and automation. The grand result: a loss of personal accountability, transparency, and the passion of scientists in discovery and development.

In the pharmaceutical business, one of the biggest disappointments of the past decade is that the sequencing of the human genome and the industrialization of techniques employed in the early discovery process have not become miracle cures for sliding R&D productivity. Indeed, the share of experimental drugs that fail in the clinical stage (when testing on people occurs) has actually risen, hitting a record 93% in 2006, according to CMR International.

The hope was that the huge amount of data from sequencing the genome would provide shortcuts in pinpointing targets for attacking diseases, and that new techniques (including combinatorial chemistry for creating new compounds and high-throughput screening for testing the medicinal potential of compounds) would allow researchers to produce safe and effective therapies much faster. But for the most part, the sequencing of the genome has provided only an alphabet; we still do not understand how to assemble the letters to form words and sentences. And the tools themselves are no substitute for first-rate scientific minds; a fool with a tool is still a fool.

How can Big Pharma's R&D problems be solved? Here are some ideas.

Redesign the Organization

By and large, pharmaceutical companies have maintained an organizational setup that worked well in the 1960s: a pyramid with functional silos (chemistry, pharmacology, clinical development, and others) all joining at the top. However, back in the 1960s the largest players employed only about 1,000 scientists each; the pyramid contained only a few management layers; there were fewer projects; scientists worked together on one campus; and resource allocation was relatively straightforward. Something happened on the way to the new century. Employment multiplied by 20. The pyramid became a monster and everything suffered. Silos could not communicate seamlessly. Overly complex matrix teams were created to try to overcome the rigidities. The decision-making process slowed. And middle and upper managers lost their command of the fast-evolving science.

In the late 1990s I concluded that the organizational pyramid had become obsolete and decided to break it into a constellation of highly focused centers of excellence designed to improve transparency, increase the speed of decision making, and restore freedom of action to the scientists actually conducting the research. GSK now has 12 centers. Each is focused on a family of related diseases (for example, Alzheimer's and other neurological diseases, or diabetes and obesity), has a CEO with the authority to initiate and kill projects, and contains a few hundred scientists from all the crucial disciplines. There are only two or three management layers between each center's CEO and key bench scientists.

The lessons learned in breaking the R&D pyramid into a constellation are many. The centers must be built around two things: a specific mission (such as discovering the most effective therapies for Alzheimer's and other neurological diseases) and the stage of the R&D process required to perform that mission (such as the choice of a particular target for attacking the disease). Anything that is not critical to the core mission and R&D process must occur outside the center of excellence. This means that all other functions—toxicology, drug metabolism, formulation, and so on—indispensable though they might be, must become service units. Leaders of these units must be selected for their ability to deliver an effective service at the lowest possible cost, which should be regularly benchmarked. We compare their performance to that of outside organizations selling the same services for a profit. This new construct has enabled us to adopt a make-versus-buy approach. Finally, the roof of the old pyramid—the functional senior vice presidents—and any other vestiges of the silo organization should be eliminated.

Their responsibilities should be distributed throughout the decentralized organization.

Improve the Quality of Leadership

The R&D process is grueling and discouraging. Most projects fail, and few scientists ever experience the thrill of producing a successful new drug. Drug discovery and development is a team sport, with moments of brilliant thinking and hours of painstakingly detailed work. In such a difficult environment, inspiring and nurturing leaders who are also accomplished scientists is indispensable.

R&D organizations, however, have traditionally promoted their best scientists to management positions—sometimes without paying enough attention to leadership abilities. Complexity and the leadership void have given rise to teams that focus too much on process and too little on producing meaningful results, and have allowed sleepwalkers and nine-to-fivers to hide in the pyramid.

Recognizing that every project needs a strong leader, we have aggressively embarked on a program to build a cadre of exceptionally gifted individuals. Such leaders are fairly easy to spot. They love the science, show passion in their desire to win, have the resilience to soldier on in the face of multiple setbacks, and genuinely care about the members of their teams. These inspiring *product finders* typically represent less than 1% of the entire R&D population, but their value is exponentially greater. They must be identified, protected, and supported.

Launch a Cultural Revolution

When I was a graduate student in pharmacology at the University of Louis Pasteur in the late 1960s and early 1970s, my thesis directors were two eminent scientists who would often review my work on a Monday. Come most Fridays, I descended into a panic because I was convinced that I had not produced anything worthy that week to show them. I then literally lived in the lab through the weekend, desperate to come up with something that might impress them. I even had a bed in the lab. That is the kind of engagement and passion I want all our scientists to share. We need every one of them to be consumed by the desire to win against all odds, to make a difference.

Such a culture existed in drug companies 50 or 60 years ago, before they became giants. But restoring it is going to take a revolution. Frankly, I think it's our biggest challenge, because scientists are a unique breed: They are nonconformists; they care much more about external recognition than money; and they tend to tune out the rest of the world. So even though their awareness that not all is well has been raised by numerous staff reductions in R&D and beyond and by questions about Big Pharma's long-term survival, that's not nearly enough.

At GlaxoSmithKline we've overhauled our incentives in R&D. We've tailored the bonus system to reward scientists for what *they* do, not what the rest of the company does. For example, when a potential drug reaches the proof-of-concept stage (its efficacy and safety have been proved), it triggers a significant payout to the core team of discoverers. We also give handsome rewards to scientists for solving major problems—such as figuring out how to make a previously insoluble drug soluble. Why do this if scientists aren't especially driven by money? Because I'll do anything that makes even a little difference. If someone convinces me that serving beer in the parking lot at five o'clock every afternoon will help attract and retain good scientists and get them to work harder, I'll do it.

My belief is that only when the right leaders are in place will the right culture emerge. R&D leaders must restore a sense of purpose to every project team, while requiring engagement, accountability, and transparency. They must establish inspiring objectives (it's all about the patient and conquering the disease) that motivate people every day, every hour, in every cubicle, in every lab. Project teams must be empowered, and their progress (or lack thereof) must be made visible to all. Success must be celebrated and generously rewarded. Poor performers should no longer be shuffled from project to project. To make our scientists feel that they have skin in the game, resource allocation must be reinvented so that teams have to compete for funding.

In short, we've got an enormous amount of work to do. At GSK we have planted a lot of seeds, but the flowers have yet to bloom.

Overhaul R&D Processes

I have two radical ideas for changing R&D processes. One—separating R&D for first-in-class drugs from that for best-in-class drugs—is in progress at GlaxoSmith-Kline. The other—something I call "the progressive blockbuster"—would require a reinvention of the clinical stage of R&D for breakthrough drugs and is just a notion at this point.

Separating First in Class from Best in Class

The R&D organization of a major pharmaceutical company typically pursues two objectives: to be first in class by discovering new targets and disease mechanisms and producing a breakthrough medicine, and to come up with the best-in-class compound for attacking a validated disease target. Currently, the pursuits of these objectives are intertwined in most R&D organizations. That is a mistake, because the requirements and risks of the first objective differ radically from those of the second. A significant means of improving R&D productivity in the short term is the intelligent separation and optimization of these two distinct activities.

To be first in class means to go where no one has ever gone before. Truly understanding the fundamental pathology of a disease requires resources, concentration, and the building of institutional knowledge and competence over a long period of time—as long as 25 years. From an economic standpoint this is by far our riskiest venture, because it involves pioneering work in biology (to discover a new target), in chemistry (to find the right compound), and in drug development and approval (to make the chemical safe and effective and to gain approval in an area where regulators lack established guidelines or rules). Despite considerable efforts,

Big Pharma has had limited success in the first-in-class arena. When we do succeed, however, it enhances our standing with payers, patients, and external constituencies. When all is said and done, curing disease is our raison d'être. Without the discovery of first-in-class drugs, Big Pharma would lose its soul.

Once a target for attacking a disease has been validated, the race is on to discover and develop the best-in-class molecule to attack it. Time is of the essence; chemistry is king; experimental biology is irrelevant. The objective is to optimize the molecule—to develop a better mousetrap. Pfizer's Lipitor, which for years has been the uncontested best statin, was the fifth statin discovered. Because the search for a best-in-class medicine does not involve breaking new ground in biology or in drug development and approval, it is much less risky than a first-in-class program but has the same—or sometimes even greater—financial rewards.

By intertwining the processes for pursuing first in class with those for pursuing best in class, we have been demanding that R&D try to perform as a ballet dancer and a football player at the same time. We end up with low productivity in both pursuits, which is a major reason why Big Pharma organizations rarely discover truly novel molecules and have become slow followers in finding best-in-class compounds on a consistent basis.

The clear separation of these activities *where possible* (complete separation is impossible) will require a significant retooling and redesign of industry efforts. For first-in-class R&D we must select many fewer endeavors, concentrate our resources, staff the effort with true discoverers, intensify our partnerships with leading academic centers, place bets on novel approaches through venture-capital-like investments, and stay on course decades or longer to succeed.

To optimize best-in-class R&D, several activities need to be strengthened. The ranks of the chemists should be reinforced, and they should be supplied with cutting-edge tools such as structure relation analysis, a software program that can help find the best candidate for a medicine from among thousands of compounds. The capability to conduct rigorous patent reviews should be improved to help teams navigate their fields of research.

Untangling the two processes will require R&D to rethink its organizational setup, allocation of resources, recruitment, culture, scorecard, and incentive systems. I fully understand that all this is much easier said than done. One especially big challenge will be deciding what to separate and what to keep together in order to minimize the duplication of functions. Although it's clear that processes and resources supporting first-in-class and best-in-class projects should be separate in the start-up phase, that's not the case further along. For example, the point at which a new target becomes a validated target is often ambiguous. And to make the best possible use of the thousands of people participating in a clinical program, first-in-class and best-in-class projects should share them. Such realities illustrate the execution challenges related to this process transformation.

As difficult as the untangling will be, it will be worth the effort. As we've seen in those centers of excellence where GSK has taken this step, the successful execution of this new model will produce a significant uplift in R&D productivity.

The Progressive Blockbuster

This idea would involve abandoning pursuit of the instant blockbuster in order to first target a limited segment of potential patients and then expand to other segments over time.

Traditionally, new drugs with potential for treating a common disease or condition such as diabetes or high cholesterol have been tested on a large, diverse patient population in clinical trials. If the trials produced the expected results and the FDA approved the drug, the result was an "instant blockbuster." However, it is common for a drug to cause side effects in a small segment of the target population. Years ago these side effects would often go undetected until *after* the drug was on the market and millions of patients had used it. Today the FDA requires companies to try to identify rare or unexpected side effects before a product launch; this has led to a record number of initial rejections and, as a result, delays in introducing new drugs.

A solution would be to begin by limiting the clinical trials to a highly uniform segment of patients—those who, for example, have a specific genetic profile or suffer from exactly the same concomitant conditions, such as diabetes and cardiovascular disease. If testing produced good results, the company could seek the FDA's approval for marketing the drug to that segment only. This approach would reduce the likelihood that rare or unexpected side effects went undetected during clinical trials and would make it easier to monitor the drug's performance after launch. Development of the drug should continue in the same way: A second uniform patient segment should be chosen. And so on.

Such systematic clinical development would address society's low tolerance for surprises (side effects in even a tiny subset of patients) and should simplify and speed up product development. Ultimately, everyone would win.

Capture Cost Efficiencies

Companies can leverage their huge R&D budgets by reducing waste and improving the quality of decision making. One area in which the opportunity for savings is huge is Phase II and Phase III clinical trials, which test the safety and efficacy of drugs on the targeted patient groups. By switching 50% of its trials from high-cost places such as the United States and Western Europe to low-cost places such as India and South America, a midsize pharmaceutical company with 60,000 patients in clinical trials could save $600 million annually. (A top-notch academic medical center in India charges $1,500 to $2,000 per patient case report, while a second-rate center in the United States charges $20,000.)

Offshoring management of clinical trial data and using IT to automate parts of the clinical trial process would also generate significant savings, and there are many other ways to cut costs as well. The key to identifying and capturing the biggest opportunities is to strengthen

R&D organizations in the way I've described above: by devolving power to strong project teams that are staffed by people who know the most about the work, are supported by a culture that empowers leaders, and are guided by a transparent and science-based framework for making decisions. Decisions tainted by wishful thinking or unduly influenced by bureaucratic or political considerations constitute one of the most wasteful elements of the R&D process and must be vigorously attacked.

Place More Bets

Improving R&D productivity alone won't be enough to save Big Pharma. Given their enormous need for new products, companies are going to have to place more bets. This will require them to change their business model so that they can increase R&D funding. The industry has been investing about 16% of revenues in R&D for the past 10 years. In view of the "all or nothing" consequences of R&D success, it seems prudent (and competitively advantageous) to raise the stakes gradually. The funding of this expansion should be made possible by shrinking an oversize selling and marketing machine. The best companies have already started on this quest.

At the same time, companies must forge alliances with academia and biotech companies. The model of a company concentrating its R&D resources inside its four walls is obsolete. Big Pharma players can no longer hope to generate the absolutely best science in all areas on their own. Therefore, standard operating procedure should be to decide on a scientific bet (for example, kinases in oncology), shop around among all the external players that are pursuing such research, and establish a contractual relationship with the best. The CEOs of our centers of excellence have the power to decide what to do inside and outside. At the end of the day we judge them on what's in their pipelines, regardless of the source.

An open architecture for R&D projects has many advantages. It forces competition between internal and external scientific teams as well as between different approaches to a common therapeutic solution. It makes the enterprise more flexible, allowing it to cancel programs without having to go through painful restructuring. In order to operate in this fashion, however, companies will need to strengthen and expand their ability to evaluate opportunities, negotiate deals, and nurture external scientific bets on a large scale—in other words, to act like a venture capitalist with in-depth understanding of the science at stake.

The innovation malaise in the pharmaceutical industry is not unique. Many other industries face the same challenges. The scientific revolution is visible to us all, but its translation into significant goods and services remains a distant goal for most large, established corporations. So instead of waiting for the scientific revolution to save us, we must rebuild our R&D engines. In most cases a cultural shift and a broad transformation of the organization are necessary first steps. This is an enormous task. In pharmaceuticals only the very best players will be able to meet the challenge and rebuild their R&D engines. The approaching wave of patent expirations leaves them little time.

JEAN-PIERRE GARNIER is the CEO of GlaxoSmithKline.

Originally published in May 2008. Reprint R0805D

Community Relations 2.0

*by Gerald C. Kane, Robert G. Fichman,
John Gallaugher, and John Glaser*

IN 2003, BOSTON UNIVERSITY Medical Campus (BUMC) announced plans to build an advanced high-security laboratory to study virulent biological agents. Stakeholders expected the lab to conduct groundbreaking research leading to public health and counterterrorism advances that would combat weaponized versions of Ebola, tularemia, anthrax, and other lethal diseases. At first, the project was widely hailed as a boon to national security, to the region's standing as a biotech leader, and to Boston's economy.

And then suddenly the tide turned. Known officially as the National Emerging Infectious Diseases Laboratories, the facility was sited near BUMC at the junction of Boston's residential South End and Roxbury neighborhoods. The more residents heard about the kinds of substances their new neighbor would handle, the less eager they were to have the building in their midst. How secure would it be? What if something got out?

Wouldn't the lab be a high-profile target for terrorists? If it was as safe as proponents claimed, why couldn't it be built in an affluent suburb like Brookline, Newton, or Wellesley?

In no small part, online activism drove powerful community opposition. A single-issue website, stopthebiolab.org, quickly galvanized a community of staunch resistance. Established organizations devoted to the environment, public health, and social justice (the Conservation Law Foundation, the Massachusetts Nurses Association, and Boston Mobilization, among others) used their websites to amplify the message. Lawsuits were filed, and in no time the lab went from slam dunk to slog. The facility's opening has been delayed by a federal court order for further environmental safety studies. Research may never be permitted on the most dangerous substances the lab was built to study.

Businesses and other institutions have long practiced "community outreach" to nurture positive, cooperative relationships between themselves and the public. Before the internet, firms had far more time to methodically monitor and respond to community activity. With the rise of social media, that luxury has vanished, leaving a community-management vacuum in dire need of fresh skills, adaptive tactics, and a coherent strategy. In fact, in today's hyperconnected world, a company's community has few geographical barriers; it comprises all customers and interested parties, not just local neighbors. This article, based on our research examining social media engagement at more than two dozen firms, describes the changes wrought by social media

Idea in Brief

Before the internet, organizations had far more time to monitor and respond to community activity, but that luxury is long gone, leaving them in dire need of a coherent outreach strategy, fresh skills, and adaptive tactics. Drawing on the authors' study of more than two dozen firms, this article describes the changes wrought by social media in particular and shows managers how to take advantage of them—lessons that Kaiser Permanente, Domino's, and others learned the hard way. Social media platforms enhance the power of communities by promoting deep relationships, facilitating rapid organization, improving the creation and synthesis of knowledge, and enabling robust filtering of information. The authors cite many examples from the health care industry, where social media participation is vigorous and influential. For instance, members of Sermo, an online network exclusively for doctors, used the site to call attention to and organize against insurers' proposed reimbursement cuts. And on Patients-LikeMe, where people share details about their chronic diseases and the treatments they've pursued, charts and progress curves help members visualize their own complex histories and allow comparisons and feedback among peers. As you modernize your company's approach to community outreach, you'll need to assemble a social media team equipped to identify new opportunities for engagement and prevent brand damage. Inthe most successful firms the authors studied, community management was a dedicated function, combining marketing, public relations, and information technology skills.

platforms and shows how your company can make the most of this brave new world.

What's Different About New Communities?

IT-enabled collaborative tools such as social networks, wikis, and blogs greatly increase a community's speed of formation and magnify its impact and reach. New communities come together and disperse quickly and are often led by different people at different moments. And mobile interfaces keep groups on the alert, ready to drum up information or break into action.

Communities vary widely in their purpose and membership—and in their tone, which can range from friendly and collaborative to ardently hostile. The importance of sorting out which is which—and then deciding whether and how to engage—makes the discipline of managing them a delicate and highly strategic internal capability.

Many of the social media communities we cite come from the health care industry, where participation is robust and influential. A report from Manhattan Research suggests that more than 60 million Americans are consumers of "health 2.0" resources. They read or contribute to blogs, wikis, social networks, and other peer-produced efforts, using Google as the de facto starting point. The lessons we extract here apply to online communities in other knowledge-driven fields, such as law (Divorce360), finance (Wikinvest, Marketocracy), publishing (Wikipedia, the Huffington Post), and R&D (InnoCentive, IdeaStorm).

With social media, we've moved beyond the era of stand-alone, static webpages. Today's communities actively post and vet information. Users increasingly treat these venues as their *first* stop in gathering data and forming an opinion. A recent Pew study found that nearly 40% of Americans say they have doubted a medical professional's opinion or diagnosis because it conflicted with information they'd found online. If users put that much faith in what they learn on the internet, what will they be willing to believe if members of a social media forum start trashing your organization? And are you prepared to handle it when it happens?

Social Media Capabilities

Social media platforms enhance the power of online communities in four ways: They promote deep relationships, allow fast organization, improve the creation and synthesis of knowledge, and permit better filtering of information.

Deep Relationships
Community members using social media tools and features establish multifaceted relationships that are far richer than those in earlier-generation online communities, such as discussion boards and LISTSERVs. These connections engender deep trust, as shown by the kind of information sharing that occurs among the ALS (amyotrophic lateral sclerosis), Parkinson's, and other member communities on PatientsLikeMe, an advanced online social network for patients with particular chronic diseases. Patients volunteer details about their diseases and the treatments they've pursued— including those not prescribed by their doctors. Charts and progress curves on the website help people to visualize their own complex treatment histories, allow comparisons among peer groups, and prompt members to provide feedback and advice on one another's progress.

The implications for health care are profound. Indeed, online communities are changing the way doctors provide care. When one member of the multiple sclerosis community on PatientsLikeMe studied a chart comparing his own treatment regimen with those of other MS patients, he concluded that his doctor was undermedicating him. As recounted in a *New York Times Magazine* article in March 2008, the patient, armed with printouts showing that higher doses were now mainstream practice, persuaded his doctor to increase the prescribed dosage. Doing so improved the patient's mobility in ways he had not experienced in 14 years.

Rapid Organization

Social media tools enable calls to action around common interests or upcoming events and promote the easy formation of electronic communities. Hundreds of thousands of people can be mobilized in just a few hours.

For example, the lung cancer group on Inspire (a website for communities of patients, families, and advocacy groups dealing with various diseases) quickly turned *Golf Digest*'s "What Would You Shoot?" contest into a promotional tool. The group rallied thousands of online voters to support cancer survivor John Atkinson, giving him a chance to play with three celebrities at Torrey Pines South the week before last year's U.S. Open. The foursome included *Today* coanchor Matt Lauer, who subsequently featured Atkinson on his TV show. The community's quick action allowed it to use Atkinson's compelling story to promote awareness and early screening.

Online communities are also leveraged in quick-strike lobbying efforts. Sermo (a social network exclusively for doctors) has enabled physicians to rapidly mobilize on a broad set of issues. For instance, they used it to call attention to insurers' proposed reimbursement cuts and successfully organize resistance to them. Recently, members were able to galvanize doctors against proposed health care reform, even when the American Medical Association formally supported it.

Knowledge Creation and Synthesis

Modern online communities can aggregate the knowledge generated by members into persistent documents and other artifacts that are much more useful than the disjointed discussion threads and bulletin boards of yore.

Wikipedia, a highly social environment governed by strong rules and norms, produces remarkably reliable information, despite its reputation for uneven quality. A recent study that Lara Devgan and colleagues from Johns Hopkins presented at the American College of Surgeons showed that a sample of Wikipedia medical articles did not contain a single egregious factual error. In fact, the vast majority were considered by the researchers to be appropriate references for patients.

PatientsLikeMe has taken information synthesis to a new level. For its growing ALS population (some 10% of newly diagnosed ALS patients are members), the site has aggregated patient-reported data heretofore inaccessible to the general public. Community members even band together for sophisticated research efforts.

Inspired by a report suggesting that lithium may benefit ALS sufferers, members recently launched what PatientsLikeMe cofounder Jamie Heywood described as "the first real-time, real-world open and non-blinded, patient-driven trial." Within months—rather than the years that formal studies can take—members had collected and shared data submitted by hundreds of lithium-taking ALS patients. The community's findings have thus far not substantiated the earlier study, perhaps saving other sufferers from pinning false hopes on a single report whose results have not been replicated.

Information Filtering

Harnessing the knowledge of a worldwide community of (mostly) amateurs would be worth little if there were no way for people to separate wheat from chaff. Fortunately, ever-improving categorization, search, and filtering tools make it possible to identify the most popular or helpful contributions. Think of the aggregate physician ratings by patients on sites such as Yelp and by nurses on CareSeek.

Sermo has one of the most robust filtering mechanisms we've ever seen. Doctors who write a new post on Sermo, often about a puzzling case, can append a poll question seeking input from other doctors. Members can filter contributions by time, author name, quality rating, specialty, or keywords relating to conditions, symptoms, treatments, and so forth. Thus doctors prospecting for interesting cases can readily find ones that match their expertise, and those seeking advice can quickly attract the most relevant contributors. Physicians have even used Sermo in the ER to gather input from a quorum of experts to decide on the spot how to treat acute cases.

Information filtering also helps alleviate problems of misuse in communities, such as misrepresentation and fraud, debilitating infighting and other hostilities, and abandonment of their original purpose. Although entirely eliminating such issues may be impossible, Sermo minimizes them by allowing members to assign reputation ratings to other users. It also carefully vets the medical credentials of its members.

The Community Opportunity

To many businesses, online communities look like antagonists, not would-be partners with intersecting interests. It's true that they're often formed, in part, as reactions against mainstream practices, values, and philosophies—but don't let a community's pedigree cloud your thinking about opportunities to create value. In the health care field, communities like Sermo, PatientsLikeMe, and Inspire may be the seeds of a future in which it's common practice for diverse constituents to attack shared problems together.

Consider the challenges of speed and scale. Medical knowledge tends to progress slowly through studies of clinical outcomes and other forms of research. As communities—alone or in networks—assemble large populations of patients, they can compile data showing the effects on patients not only of various medical treatments but also of age, genetics, nutrition, mental outlook, socioeconomic status, physical fitness, and the presence of other medical conditions. The ultimate opportunity is to customize treatment protocols to match ever more granular sets of patient and disease characteristics (see "Realizing the Promise of Personalized Medicine," HBR October 2007). Thus a physician would be able to assess treatment options for an individual patient against a body of experiential evidence drawn from tens of thousands of detailed cases of a particular disease—such as diabetes, HIV/AIDS, or rheumatoid arthritis.

In health care, collaboration within communities is motivated by a shared passion to spread knowledge. Patients, their physicians, and their families and friends want better treatments for whatever the disease may be. Ben and Jamie Heywood, whose brother Stephen suffered from ALS, created PatientsLikeMe to help patients share their experiences, to empower them, and to stimulate thinking that could lead to a cure.

Patient communities, unlike health care providers, can operate outside the strictures of HIPAA (the Health Insurance Portability and Accountability Act). Patients can freely share information about their conditions and treatments that a hospital or a doctor's office must keep confidential. These communities allow fee-paying partners—pharmaceutical firms, device makers, research organizations, and nonprofits—to access aggregated, anonymous member data. Partners may also recruit members as medical-trial subjects as long as individuals have given permission to be contacted.

Such novel cooperative alliances in health care should inspire similar experimentation in other industries. Like many managers, you may be dealing with outside communities mainly by trying to minimize their negative potential, but there are sure to be communities whose goals complement your own. For that reason, as you modernize your company's approach to community relations, you'll need to recognize the key distinction between two fundamental activities: preventing damage to your reputation and brand, and identifying new opportunities. The former calls for marketing and public relations skills, whereas the latter calls for business-development skills. You should assemble a social media team with strengths in both areas.

Moreover, you probably already have members of these communities within your company's walls. At Boston-based Partners HealthCare, doctors are active on Sermo, many patients belong to groups within Patients-LikeMe and Inspire, and more than 3,500 employees have joined an informal and unofficial Partners community on Facebook. These existing relationships create natural points of intersection between Partners' interests and those of relevant online communities.

Engaging the Next Generation of Online Communities

A company's social media team must develop policies and strategies for managing online communities, both to mitigate negative consequences and to foster

The Mandate for the Social Media Team

1: Develop a Formal Social Media Policy

Appropriate standards and guidelines for on-the-job use of social media by employees will make the firm's expectations clear and help govern usage. A good policy is explicit about how employees should interact in communities, giving positive examples and highlighting the possible consequences of damaging conduct. A survey of companies with formal social media policies reveals the following core guidelines:

Accountability. Employees should take responsibility for their postings, clearly indicating when opinions are their own and not the firm's.

Accuracy and transparency. Posts must be factual, with the poster's identity disclosed.

Lawfulness. Employees must be aware of and respect the legal and professional framework that governs firm behavior.

2: Monitor External and Internal Online Communities

Because communities come and go quickly, the team should continually survey the online landscape to identify potential threats and allies. Here are a few tips:

Leverage tools. Google alerts, blog trackers, Twitter keyword monitors, Facebook's Lexicon, and other simple tools can help make this daunting task more manageable.

Mobilize internal deputies. A small core team simply can't find every social media activity relevant to your company's interests. Deputized employees can augment the team's efforts, even by revealing conversations that take place in the so-called dark web (on sites, such as Facebook, where only "friends" have access).

3: Engage Online Communities

Your team should develop your firm's social media presence so that people can talk *to you*, not just *about you*. For example:

Create a compelling social media voice. Facebook fan pages and corporate blogs are engaging. Online innovation forums, like Dell's Idea Storm and Starbucks' My Starbucks Idea, also draw in the public. And when J&J subsidiary Life-Scan announced a prototype iPhone app for diabetics to monitor glucose levels, it used social media to answer questions that a simple press release could not anticipate.

Reach out to community leaders. Prominent bloggers and well-connected social-network participants can be powerful allies. You aren't trying to recruit mouthpieces; you want to gauge reaction and make sure your message is understood. The key to productive relationships with community leaders like these is to find genuine common ground. Bloggers are also often experts on the social media landscape in general. When Kaiser Permanente asked well-known health care bloggers how to begin engaging online communities, it received valuable input on crafting its social media strategy.

Be a liaison to internal communities. The social media team should be a clearinghouse for information on emerging internal communities, from a company softball league to a work-related wiki. If the team knows about these initiatives, it can steer them in productive directions, unify platforms and tools, and reward exemplary efforts.

4: Act as First Responders

Some issues require immediate action—but a rapid yet ill-conceived reaction can make matters worse. Therefore team members,

(continued)

The Mandate for the Social Media
Team (continued)

like real-world first responders, should be trained to triage situations.

Acknowledge mistakes. This is a key first step in regaining consumer trust. Customers can be forgiving if they perceive honesty in the message. When Facebook incited outrage in social media forums for its 2009 revision of its terms of service, founder Mark Zuckerberg blogged an apology: "We simply did a bad job with this release, and I apologize for it." Of course, the community will expect a good-faith effort to address the underlying problem. After apologizing, Facebook revised its terms again and asked its community to vote on them.

Ward off crises. You can't afford to let unfounded rumors spiral out of control. Earlier this year, when stories surfaced that Starbucks was protesting the Iraq war by refusing to send coffee to troops, the coffee giant fired back with "not true" tweets with links to details on its good works.

Engage selectively. An active response is not always advisable. Some online communities empower dysfunctional behavior you don't want associated with your company. For example, some communities of eating-disorder sufferers encourage destructive behavior by posting purging techniques and photos of skeletal sufferers to offer "thinspiration." Even if you don't engage, you need to be aware of such communities.

positive engagement. Its responsibilities should include monitoring online communities that exist outside and inside the company, engaging those communities when necessary, and serving as first responders in the event of a social media crisis. (For more details, see the sidebar "The Mandate for the Social Media Team.")

Those concerned about spending in an era of resource constraints should note that companies as diverse as Kaiser Permanente, Comcast, Domino's, and Amazon have learned that not having such a team can cost far more than having one. The Domino's employees who torpedoed the firm's image with a grotesque YouTube montage of intentional health code violations claimed they simply hadn't thought about the consequences of their actions.

In the most successful firms we've studied, community management was a dedicated function combining skills from marketing, public relations, and information technology. But there is no one-size-fits-all formula. A leading health care company has a single social media team reporting jointly to the VP of public relations and to the CIO. By contrast, in the video game industry (where online communities represent an especially influential customer voice), one leading company assigns a full-time community liaison to each major product offering. Liaisons serve on product-group teams and report both to the senior community manager and to a senior marketer. In all cases, direct communication between community managers and senior executives is vital. Otherwise, intermediary agents could distort critical messages—for instance, by minimizing criticism of efforts they had a hand in creating.

The social media team does not need to retain sole responsibility for engaging the social media space, however. Virtually every organization has a cadre of employees who are already active in online communities. These workers constitute a rich pool of experience, expertise, and energy that the social media team can draw from. They should be deputized to assist with the team's core mission.

Identifying these rank-and-file social media experts gives you access to key insights and, potentially, smart strategies. When Ernst & Young hired an agency to craft its college-recruiting presence on Facebook, the results were unremarkable. Only when the company enlisted a group of interns who were active Facebookers to contribute did the recruitment drive become more "authentic" and draw more traffic. *BusinessWeek* technology columnist Sarah Lacy says E&Y's Facebook presence contributed to the company's rapid rise among the magazine's rankings of top firms that college students want to work for.

It's time to take social media seriously. Comcast didn't expect that one of its snoozing technicians would become a viral video sensation and the source of widespread negative publicity. And Kaiser Permanente had no idea that a blog rant by a low-level employee could disrupt a multibillion-dollar IT rollout and end up on the front pages of the *Los Angeles Times* and the *Wall Street Journal*. Both organizations have since emerged as leaders in engaging online communities, but each learned its lesson the hard way. Luckily, you can take steps now not only to avoid costly errors but also to harness the power of online communities.

GERALD C. KANE is an assistant professor of information systems. **ROBERT G. FICHMAN** is an associate professor of information systems. **JOHN GALLAUGHER** is an associate professor of information systems at Boston College's Carroll School of Management. **JOHN GLASER** is the CIO of Partners HealthCare in Boston.

Originally published in November 2009. Reprint R0911C

Index

organizations
  basing design on needs of
    population, 46
  common set of tools and
    procedures, 81
  environment, structure, and
    history, 34–35
  first analyzing problems, 81
  rapidly disseminate and use
    new knowledge, 32
  shepherding patients through
    units, 41
  teaching employees to be-
    come experimentalists, 59
organizing to deliver high
  performance, 8–9
ossified government
  bureaucracies, 47
outcomes
  comparing, 4
  improving, 18
  measuring, 4
output, 72

Parkinson's disease, 207
Partners HealthCare System, 2,
  3, 20, 22
  financial incentives, 12
  online communities, 213
  peer pressure, 12
patent-protected drugs, 187
patients
  access to high-cost or scarce
    resources, 40
  care coordinators, 102–103
  care defined by needs, 9–10
  comparing outcomes, 4
  complex or multiple
    illnesses, 40
  complex or poorly understood
    conditions, 41

defining strategy around
  needs of, 21–22
health care disruptions,
  148–149
improving outcomes, 48
managing diabetes, 142–144
multiple interacting conditions or diseases, 32–33
optimizing care, 31, 35
separating high- and low-
  variability care, 31
PatientsLikeMe, 205, 207–213
PBMs (pharmaceutical benefit
  managers), 121
peer pressure, 3, 11–13
performance
  data, 12
  improvements in, 4–5
  matters, 3–4
  measurement, 5–6, 42
  organizing for, 7–11
  small insights and innovations
    impact, 45
  teamwork, 4–5
  unrealistically high
    standard, 12
  volume and profitability of
    services delivered, 7
personal computers and
  disruptive technologies, 141
pharmaceutical benefit
  managers. See PBMs
  (pharmaceutical benefit
  managers)
pharmaceutical companies,
  189–191
pharmaceutical industry
  academia and biotech compa-
    nies, 199–200
  acting like venture capitalist,
    200
  broad transformation, 200